VILLAGE FOLK

THE HISCOCKS : A RAMSBURY FAMILY

LOCALE Series Number 4

The Locale series enables important works of Wiltshire history to be published in an economical, but attractive format.

1. Bishopstone: a history of the farms, houses and people of a south Wiltshire village; by Elizabeth Gallop. 1988.

2. Pitton and Farley: the very joyfullest start; by Michael Parsons. 1988.

3. Snap: the history, depopulation and destruction of a Wiltshire village; by K.G. Watts. 1989.

4. Village Folk; by Len Noble. 1990.

5. The Manor of Melksham Canonhold; by Isabel Ide and Megan Watts. Autumn 1990.

Cover picture: The Hiscocks and the Ramsbury tree. Clockwise from the right, Olive, Gordon, Henry and Leonora, Sid, Gladys.

VILLAGE FOLK

THE HISCOCKS

A RAMSBURY FAMILY

Experiments in Oral History.

As told to

LEN NOBLE

by

Gordon and Sidney Hiscock, Gladys Finch

and

Olive Noble

1990

Acknowledgements

To Gordon, Sidney, Gladys and Olive, for their patient hours of talking, writing and encouraging, and without whom, this account of their life in Ramsbury and elsewhere could not have been recorded.

To my daughter-in-law Pam, who typed the first readable manuscript out of a mass of scribble.

To the Mantle Oral History Project, the Mantle Writers Workshop, for the help and facilities at Mantle Community Arts, The Springboard Centre, Coalville, Leicestershire.

To the Coalville Technical College for the first introduction to the small world of word processing!

To Steve Duckworth for initiation into the complexities of Desktop Publishing.

To John and Diana Niblett, Dave Clare and Paul Ruddle of D.A. Computers of Leicester for so much help and advice.

And to John Chandler and Michael Marshman for advice and for enabling the project to get off the ground!

Published by

Wiltshire County Council, Library & Museum Service,
Bythesea Road, Trowbridge, Wiltshire, BA14 8BS

Director: R.L. Pybus, MA, FLA, FCIS, MILAM, MBIM.

I.S.B.N. 0 86080 193 4

Printed by Wiltshire County Council

Dedication

To my wife

OLIVE

who is, to me, central to the story
and who often says

'Life was better at Ramsbury'.

CONTENTS

ILLUSTRATIONS AND MAPS

RAMSBURY

Ramsbury is a large village in north Wiltshire situated in the beautiful Kennet Valley, nearly midway between Hungerford and Marlborough. Almost untouched by progress, although once on the main coach road from London to the West, Ramsbury has missed out on railways, canals and motorways.

The village is mostly on the north bank of the river with the houses looking upward into the afternoon sun towards Spring Hill, from where part of the Normandy Invasion Force flew off in June 1944.

The woods still abound with game and the river with fish. Guarded upstream by Ramsbury Manor and downstream by Littlecote, the aristocrats, the noble and the affluent continue traditions set centuries ago. The annual cost of a rod or a gun now amounts to more than a man like Harry Hiscock could earn in a lifetime.

Ramsbury doesn't often hit the headlines. The contrast between the privacy of Harry Hyams at the Ramsbury Manor and the expansive commercialism of Peter de Savary at Littlecote with the brief sandwich of Diana Ross in the village (which she is alleged to have 'found too quiet') is all of the 'new generation'.

The ancient Bishopric of Ramsbury has only recently been restored, Littlecote has become a 'Day-out' for the family and the 'Victorian Garden' in nearby Chilton Foliat has been rescued as a television series.

The ancient hollow elm in the village square, long the playground of children, and the meeting place of generations of courting couples, has gone, its place being taken by a sapling, a not inappropriate move to mark the start of a new period of new blood.

The old village families and their way of life are fast disappearing. This account of one such family is an effort to hold fast the door before it shuts tight.

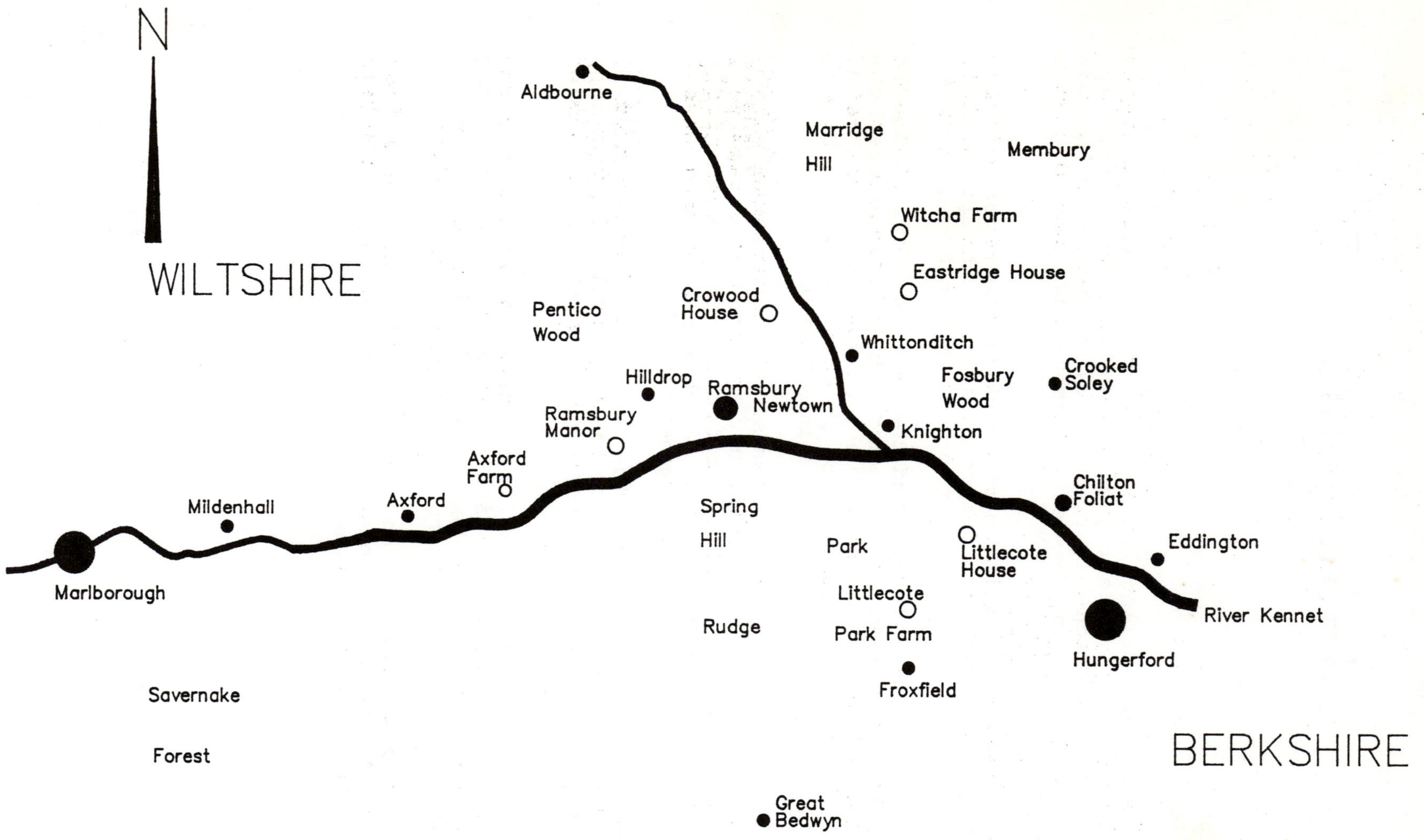

The Kennet Valley between Marlborough and Hungerford

Oxford Street looking towards The Square c1900.

Oxford Street looking towards *The Crown* c1900.

PREFACE

This is the story of a family who lived in the village of Ramsbury in the first half of the twentieth century. Told in their own words it recalls a world gone forever.

The introduction sets the scene and describes the bare outline of the establishment of the family, its gradual break up as each left the village to seek work, to establish their own families, and, finally the death of the parents. Some memories have been written down, and taped conversations at family gatherings have been transposed. For the sake of coherence, the various aspects of their childhood, fragmentary in recorded speech have been drawn together and are presented as a series of conversations. A variety of techniques has been used and there is some repetition which is left in deliberately.

'Gladys Remembers' is an edited version of Gladys' written work. The two 'Conversations' present, in short story form, fragments of real conversations, but in a village setting, while the 'Dialogues' and Gordon of 'Tonbridge' are edited versions of taped conversations. The 'Postscript' rounds off the final involvement with Ramsbury.

Delamere
Ellistown
Leicester

Len Noble

THE FAMILY

Henry Hiscock was born in 1868 at Oare, a small village just south of Marlborough in Wiltshire, on the edge of the Vale of Pewsey. His father George, who was born about 1830, came from a family who had long lived in the same locality working on the land. His mother, Eliza (Smith), came from nearby Wilcot.

George and Eliza had a large family, five sons and six daughters. They were Caleb, David, Henry, Walter and George, Elizabeth, Fanny, Mary, Janet, Louisa and Jessie. Mary was always called Pol, Henry was called Harry and George (junior) was called Tommy. There is no record of Caleb after the age of twenty-one when the census shows him working as a groom for the vicar of Huish. David became landlord of the White Hart in Oare, Henry was apprenticed at the age of twelve to a blacksmith, Walter worked mostly away from the village but returned to the area later in life. Tommy not only remained in the village all his life but also lived in the house where he was born. A well respected figure he was sexton for 29 years. All the girls married and their families live in Australia, the United Kingdom and Canada. Jessie married Alfred Beckingham who worked on a nearby farm, emigrated with her five children to Western Australia in 1913, where after many years of hardship they became large-scale farmers. Her descendants now number over fifty and some still farm in the Wheat Belt of Western Australia. Until 1987 contact with the Australian family had been lost, but thanks to the Wiltshire Family History Society, firm contact has been restored through the combined efforts of George and Eliza Hiscock's great granddaughters, Joan Steele in Australia, and Olive in England. How long Harry stayed at Oare is not known, but it was there that he learnt his trade, and it seems probable that he must have shod horses for his Uncle Maurice who farmed nearby.

At some stage Harry moved to Eddington, along the Great West Road, close to Hungerford. There he was a blacksmith in the steel-works, and it was there that he met and married Leonora Eliza Hobbs.

Henry Hiscock was a country boy, Wiltshire born and bred. Miss Hobbs was quite different. She was a girl from the town, and, what's more "Up-country"! Leonora came from Richmond in Surrey, the youngest of six children, her father was a coachman and her mother, Sarah Ann, had been a dressmaker. At about the time of Leonora's birth in 1872, her parents, Henry and Sarah Ann, parted and Leonora was brought up by "Aunt Mary" at Richmond. She was given a good education and it was intended that she should become a teacher. But, before this could happen, she was transferred to another aunt living at Hungerford.

Aunt Harriet was married to Mark Tidbury who sold tea and insurance! Close by the Tidbury house was the steel-works where Harry Hiscock was blacksmith.

Harry and Leonora married in October 1897. Harry was twenty-eight and Leonora twenty-five. It is thought that Harry may have worked for Taskers at Andover at some time but it was not long before he became blacksmith at Osmond's Foundry at Ramsbury and Harry and Leonora set up house at number two Mount Pleasant in Blind Lane (now Union Street) in Ramsbury. Mount Pleasant was a terrace of six flint and brick cottages, set high on a bank, at right angles to the road and facing south across the Kennet valley towards Spring Hill. The house was two up and two down with no water other than a communal well on the bank by the lane, and only candles or paraffin lamps for light. There was one fireplace. The closets of rough-sawn, waney-edged boards were set in pairs down the garden. Not exactly a paradise, but the view across the thatched roof of the house in front was magnificent! And well it might be, for it was to be the main view for Harry and Leonora for the rest of their lives.

In that house Leonora had six children. Three boys and three girls, between 1901 and 1914. One boy, Arthur, died in infancy, but Hilda May (1901), Gordon Henry (1905), Sidney Ernest (1910), Gladys Marjorie (1911) and Doris Esme (1914) spent all their childhood in Ramsbury.

Harry, a highly-skilled craftsman, worked hard at the Foundry. In peacetime, making and repairing farm machinery, and forging, welding and shaping all manner of things in the fire. Arc-welding and gas-cutters were not in common use. Whether the job was forging a new plough-share or servicing the huge traction engines that were then used for ploughing and threshing, Harry Hiscock was the man. No job, where metal was involved, was too big or too small. But this was also the age of the horse and Harry was a farrier as well as a blacksmith and there were always horses waiting to be shod.

In the Great War Harry was briefly called to the Colours, but Osmonds found that they could not tackle the rush of Government contracts and so Harry was released by the Army and sent back to the Foundry.

After the Great War the dark days of the Agricultural Depression of the 1920s and 1930s began to affect the rural economy. Work and money were short. It became necessary for Harry to take on odd jobs after working hours. One day Wilsons, who now owned the Foundry, told Harry that he was too old to be kept on. By then the Unemployment Act had brought the Dole (and the Means Test) and, with luck, its provisions might last out until the Old Age Pension.

But Harry was a proud man. A living had to be earned and so the odd jobs multiplied. Whether it was cutting reeds in the river in the summer or beating for the shoots in the winter, Harry was there. And, in between, pot-mending, soldering and a dozen other things.

Leonora, with a large family to care for, was fully occupied, cooking on the tiny open kitchen range, washing the sheets and clothes in the tin bath and sewing, always sewing, on the treadle sewing machine for family and neighbours. And there were always letters to write for someone. There were men away at war, to the Falklands and Patagonia (where some young men spent years as shepherds), applications for jobs, forms to fill in, letters to emigrant relatives; whatever it was Leonora provided a social service.

In the long years of the tens, twenties and thirties, money at Mount Pleasant was often short, but the children were always clean, well-mannered and well fed. Leonora passed on her skills of reading and writing to her children so that all were far above average. The two boys Gordon and Sidney, with their father, were adept at living off the land. The cottage larder was supplemented with rabbits, hares, pheasants and partridges; plover and moorhen eggs, fish from the river and, very occasionally, venison. But that was only when they happened to kill a deer in the park, or perhaps one that had strayed from the forest.

In 1922 their first grandchild was born at Mount Pleasant. The eldest daughter, Hilda May, had married Henry George Westall from Aldbourne. The Westalls and Henry George's mother Sarah (Wootton) had deep roots in both villages.

After the birth of the baby the new family moved to The Butts at Aldbourne. But the marriage was short-lived. Henry George had been badly wounded in the Great War, had contracted tuberculosis and by 1923 was dead. Hilda May had to return to work and the baby, Olive Norah, was returned to Mount Pleasant to be reared by Harry and Leonora as one of their family.

The post Great War years of the Depression affected not only the aging Harry, there was no work in the village for school-leavers either. There were few jobs where the young worker could live at home. There was either farm work where the "chap" could live-in and be at the farmer's beck and call twenty four hours a day or, particularly for girls, the social slavery of domestic service. The chances of further education after leaving the village school were theoretical. Deprivation and isolation ruled. But, in spite of all, the days of childhood for the family were long and happy.

The last of Harry and Leonora's grandchildren to attend the village school were Sid's daughters June and Madeleine, who travelled daily from Southside Cottage at Axford, and Gladys' boys John and Gerald Finch who were 'evacuated' with their mother to Mount Pleasant during World War Two.

Gradually all the Hiscock children, except Doris, left the village. Hilda May married again and lived in Swindon. Gordon Henry left in 1927 to work in Kent, marry and raise a large family. Sidney Ernest stayed at home while he worked in the gardens at the Manor and at Rosier's, the grocers in Oxford Street, but when he married the keeper's daughter from Park they set up house, first at Whittonditch then later at Axford. Gladys Marjorie too moved away, married a Marine and returned only briefly to Ramsbury during the Second World War. Olive left home before the outbreak of war to work first at Marlborough College and then later in Kent. She married a soldier and, with her family, moved back into the Parish of Ramsbury. After four years she too moved to Devon.

Harry died in 1948 followed within a few years by Leonora. They lie buried in the cool shade of the tall beech tree in Ramsbury Churchyard.

Not long after Doris moved away.

Number two Mount Pleasant, which some might say had been Leonora's prison, was empty. Confining it may have been, but in no way was it a prison. To Leonora the house which had, for half a century, been full of the happiness and bustle of her large family had been her whole world.

The family that Harry and Leonora raised at Mount Pleasant always speak of that house as home and Ramsbury as 'their village'. It is the main topic of conversation when they meet and it is on these memories that this story is based.

GLADYS REMEMBERS

DAD, MY SISTERS, OLIVE, THE RIVER AND THE FOUNDRY

"I was born at number two, Mount Pleasant, Ramsbury, Wiltshire on November 13th 1911. Mother's name was Leonora Eliza, and father's was Henry. Henry Hiscock, but mostly he was called 'Harry'. He was a blacksmith at Osmond's Foundry down Newtown. I was fourth of five children. There was Hilda the eldest, then Gordon, Sidney and my younger sister Doris. There was an older brother who died as a child, before I was born.

We were all born at Mount Pleasant, a tiny flint and red brick cottage in Blind Lane. Although there was no traffic in the Lane, apart from farm carts, Dad slotted some planks of wood across the door to keep us from wandering off. I used to have to look after Doris, a very nervous child who would cry at the slightest thing.

My very earliest memory was during the Great War. I remember mother putting shirts and socks and bread and cheese into a knapsack for my father, who had been called-up. Before he left he kissed us all goodbye and mother cried. It was the first time I had ever seen her cry. We asked what was wrong and she told us that there was a war with Germany and that father had to go away. I don't remember how long he was away, but he was soon back home because Mr Osmond needed him at the foundry to help make things for the forces.

I spent a lot of time watching father rivet water tanks and casting all manner of farm machinery parts such as plough shares and roller rings. As they took the red hot castings from the mould he would use a small pair of bellows to cool the iron saying "Gently does it! Now gently does it!"

In the foundry yard there were greengage trees which we loved to climb to get at the unripe fruit, only to be rewarded with the belly ache!

Father worked hard from first light till dusk and was always doing extra jobs, in what little spare time he had left, such as pot-mending or anything to do with metal.

Once, the parson, the Reverend Wellesley-Orr, a very tall man was succeeded by the Reverend Shuttleworth, a much shorter man. The church lectern had to be modified and Dad took on the work. While he was doing the job the lectern stood for some time in the pantry at Mount Pleasant! Father never refused a job. When the weeds in the River Kennet had to be cleared, Dad would help with the scything. I didn't like to see the water-lilies go but a bonus was the fish that were caught and shared among the workers. I suppose I learned to scale and gut a fish almost as soon as I could paunch and skin a rabbit.

Although my father was a highly skilled and industrious man, like so many more in those days, he never received a fair wage for his efforts. Money was always short and every household needed a good manager like my mother.

Things were so bad that many people couldn't cope and had to rely on charity or the parish. I once asked mother why we were poor and she replied that although we were poor, we were not so poor as some, and, that in any case we were the "genteel" poor. I knew what she meant!

My eldest sister was a very attractive girl and boys were always pestering to go out with her. Sometimes they would wait for her at the bottom of the court and, as I was ten years younger than she was, I was often sent to find out which one it was who fancied his chances! Hilda worked away from home most of the time, but when she did come home she spent hours and hours dress-making and altering clothes. She was very fussy about her appearance and was always washing and ironing. She even ironed her shoe laces!

When I was about nine or ten Hilda married George Westall from Aldbourne, who was a postman. He had served in the Great War and had been quite badly wounded. My parents were not too happy with the match; they were anxious on account of his health. However, Hilda and George first lived at Mount Pleasant but after their daughter, Olive, was born, they moved to Aldbourne about three miles away. George's health gradually worsened and he was sent to a sanatorium in Surrey. Within a month or so he was dead. He was given a military funeral at Aldbourne and Hilda and Olive came back to live with us at Ramsbury. Of course Hilda had to go back to work and Olive was brought up as our sister. That meant that mother now expected me to look after both Doris and Olive!

Olive had been born with a 'broad thumb'. She used to keep it tucked out of sight under her fingers and would often look at it and say 'Naughty thumb!' I suppose in these days a small operation would correct it, but in those days small things were not bothered with, which is a pity.

When Olive was two or three years old she had a mastoid abscess and was taken by car to Savernake Hospital. She was quite ill and my brothers used to cycle seven or eight miles to see her. I sometimes went on Mabel Westall's carrier wagonette to Marlborough and walked up the hill to the hospital.

We were not allowed into the ward and could only look at her through a little window. She used to get very upset; I think now that it might have been better if we had stopped away. She was very ill and it was weeks before she was allowed home.

Another time she had pleurisy and had to be operated on so she didn't have much luck did she?"

ABOUT THE HOUSE

"Mother was always busy, writing letters for people or stitching away on her old Singer treadle sewing machine either dressmaking or doing alterations. She received very little payment for it all. Like dad, she too was industrious and brought us all up the same way. We each had our jobs to do. Mine was to clean the steel fender and fire irons; I first used emery paper and then finished off with Silvo. When the kettle boiled over or even spat it would start the rust marks all over again. It was an endless job. Knives too were cleaned on an emery board, the stairs and the kitchen table scrubbed white, the fire-grate black leaded and the hearth whitened with bath-brick. I quite enjoyed black-leading and, after leaving and going into service it was the one job I still did when I came home. In later years the stairs were carpeted, so that saved one job!

Our cottage was owned by Mr Hobbs, who lived up the street. The rent was two shillings and sixpence and he collected it every Saturday morning. He never did any repairs or painting, and paperhanging was done by us. There was linoleum on the damp brick floors and a cloth peg-rug on the hearth. With an open kitchen range there was always plenty of dust about. But I quite liked dusting and polishing, at least you could see something for your efforts!

The day I disliked most of all was Mondays.

Mondays was wash day, wet or fine!

Clothes for washing were collected, sorted into various piles and washed in a zinc bath. Sheets and pillow-cases were boiled in a big black pot over the fire. There were no detergents, just Sunlight soap and soda. Soap powder came later. The first I can remember was Rinso. When the clothes had boiled they were taken out of the pot by twisting them round a long wooden copper-stick and then put into a bath to rinse. We used endless buckets of water which we had to draw from the well. The final rinse always had a good squeeze of blue-bag.

Monday washday dinner was always the same!

Cold meat from Sunday's roast, mashed potatoes and pickles!

After dinner we cleared up the wash pots and put them away for another week under the stairs in the pantry. Then the lino was washed and the hearth-rug put down. It would be four o'clock before the room was ship-shape again.

We girls did the ironing. The steel flat irons were stood in a row close to the fire so that, as the one in use cooled, there was always another one to take its place. There was always so much to do and so little time. Washday then was a full day's work."

Henry and Leonora Hiscock
at Mount Pleasant.

Mark and Maud Skerry
at Mount Pleasant.

Henry Hiscock in his garden, with Carolyn Noble
in the pram, at Mount Pleasant.

THE CONVENIENCES

"These days they'd be called 'inconveniences', but then, everyone had the same system.

There was no tap indoors. The well.at the side of the first cottage, just by the steep gravel path that led up from Blind Lane, served all six cottage. Each house had its own bucket to hook on to the rope at the well-top. There were tin baths kept under each rain-water spout between each pair of cottages, and the water was used for laundry and more particularly, for washing our hair. It was so soft that we rarely used shampoo. That is, except for my sister Hilda. She always used Amami which they used to sell under the slogan 'Friday night's Amami night!'

At the bottom of the Lane there was a pump which provided water for cooking. In the winter the pump was very often frozen up and we would have to take a kettle of hot water to unfreeze it. Just as soon as the pump was unfrozen and could be heard working, the neighbours would come running with their buckets!

There was no drainage or sanitation in the houses. If ever we girls wanted to have a wash down we would have to shut ourselves in the pantry after the boys had gone out. All the waste water was carried out through the living room into the garden. The closets were built in twos, semi-detached you might say, at the bottom of the garden. Ours was next to Mr and Mrs Giddings'.

There was only a thin partition between the closets and we always knew when Grand-dad Giddings was in theirs because we could smell his tobacco smoke! If ever I happened to be in our closet when he came down to use theirs I would always sit very still until he had gone! And then, eventually, when I went indoors mother would grumble at me for being a long time!

The good old standby was then, as it sometimes is today, especially on cold wet winter nights, the chamber pot!

There was no privacy anywhere, neither in the house, nor in the bog!"

THE NEIGHBOURS

"Immediate neighbours, especially in a terrace block, tend to be more prominent in one's memories than anyone else in the village. Our neighbours at Mount Pleasant were part of our everyday lives.

At number one lived Mr and Mrs Giddings, an elderly couple. Mrs Giddings was always known as 'Ria'. This was probably short for 'Maria' but to us kids she was 'Granny' Giddings. They both relied a great deal on our family and, more especially, on my mother. They were good people but whenever Granny Giddings was in trouble and wanted help, she would bang on the chimney breast with the poker! We always went round, straight away, to see what she wanted. We children ran all her errands but mother warned us never to accept anything in return ... but, sometimes, unbeknown to her, we would take a ha'penny! Mother wrote all their letters, filled in various forms and, every week, packed up the Marlborough Times for their daughter in America.

As a small child I was not too well behaved, and I think that I caused my mother a great deal of worry. I remember that I liked to eavesdrop on adult conversation. Once, when my mother was talking to Granny Giddings next door, I sat on the doorstep, listening.

I heard my mother say, referring to me, 'I don't know what I'm going to do with her! She won't do anything she's told! She never comes when she's called, and she always stays out later than she's supposed to!'

This brought a sharp retort from Granny Giddings.

'Nora!' she said, 'Don't worry too much gal! It's the wild colts that makes the tame hosses!'

In later years when I was nursing my mother in her final illness, she recalled the conversation and said 'So Granny Giddings' words came true!' Until that moment my mother had been unaware that I had heard what had been said all those years before!

The gardens at Mount Pleasant were in front of the houses and the Giddings' kept a pig and chickens in theirs. All the neighbours saved their small potatoes and vegetable peelings to feed them. The swill was boiled up by Mr Giddings down the bottom of the garden where he had an old pot on a make-shift grate of a few iron bars on some bricks. The pig-killer lived in Oxford Street. he was a big man with a big thirst, but he never got drunk. They always used to say that the secret of this was that he kept a bag of raisins in his pocket and these he'd chew all day long so that the booze never affected him!

On pig-killing day Mr Giddings would boil up great quantities of water to scald the pig, and the pig-killer would set up his trestle. There was always much squealing but the job was soon done. The neighbours' return for their potatoes and peelings was pig's 'fry'.

That name covered the offal, things like lights, liver, heart, spleen and gut-fat but never kidneys. Later on we might get a basin of home-cured lard. The Giddings always had a side of bacon hanging from the rafters in the living-room. Food hygiene was minimal! There was all that dust from the open fire and the flies had to be kept at bay by the fly-papers that swung stickily from the ceiling. I think that at one time Mr Giddings had been a woodman at Littlecote or Crowood.

As I've said, we lived at number two, Henry Hiscock, blacksmith and family.

At number three lived Mr and Mrs Hall and their family. Mr Hall was a distinguished looking man with a grey beard. After Mr Hall died their daughter Maud, who was married to Mark Skerry, lived there. Mark was one of those who had worked in Patagonia and the Falklands as a young man. They had four children, Fred, Frank, Reg and Ivy. It was quite a lot for a small house but I think that they had another house at the top of Blind Lane where Mark slept.

In number four lived Mr and Mrs Brown and Bob. Mr Brown was another of the men who had been working in Patagonia.

At number five, Mr and Mrs Vokins. They kept pigeons and cats. Two boxes of pigeons were brought out of the house every morning and hung on hooks on the front wall. Every night they were taken back into the pantry. We never could count exactly how many cats they had. Every stray found its way to their door. They were in every chair, on the table and she always had one on her lap. In her back bedroom she had piles and piles of old newspapers and magazines. She would loan these to us, a few at a time. She always counted how many we had borrowed, so we had to be careful to take all of them back. I can remember reading *Murder in the Red Barn* in one of them but mother wasn't too happy about us reading such 'trash'. She wanted us to read 'proper' books.

Some Sundays we would go up to Mrs Vokins' on the pretext of wanting to borrow a magazine. What we really went for was in the hope of being offered a slice of suet pudding. Mrs Vokins cooked everything in one pot suspended on a hook over the fire. She had nets for vegetables and bacon, with the suet pudding in a cloth. If we were lucky we would get a slice of suet pudding with brown sugar on it! It didn't matter a jot to us about the unique flavour and we ate it quite happily. Mother didn't like us doing this at all! She said that the pudding might have cats hairs in it and, that in any case, it would spoil our dinner.

In the end house lived Mrs Rose and her son Alfred. When anybody in the village died Mrs Rose laid them out. 'Liza' Rose she was called and her son was a very tall loose-limbed chap. A gangling great man."

FRIENDS

"My brothers, Gordon and Sid, were real out-door country boys and would always be off with other boys like Fred and Frank Hall rabbiting or up to some prank. Apart from Maud, who lived next door, two of my friends were Dora and Joan Westall. Their mother was the local carrier and she drove the wagonette regularly to Marlborough and Hungerford, delivering parcels and people and always doing the shopping as required. She had two horses called Major and Wilson. Some evenings in the summer we took them grass-baiting along the side of the road. We would ride them home but, one evening, some boys came up behind with sticks and frightened them. Off they went at a gallop with us holding on as well as we could! Up Elmdown Hill and they didn't stop for ages. They went right through the brambles and we got scratched hands and faces and, worse, we lost our hair ribbons!

Sometimes on a Sunday, Dad would hire the wagonette from Mrs Westall and drive us all over to Oare, the village where he was born. We had to start away very early in the morning to arrive by dinner time. Two or three uncles lived at Oare and Uncles Tommy and Frank lived side by side at Vine Cottages. We always had a good time on those days and we'd talk about it for ages afterwards.

Another friend was Laura Mildenhall. Her family had a wind-up gramophone and our favourite record was 'Only Make Believe' from 'Showboat'. I can never hear that tune now but it brings back memories ... Laura and I walked miles and miles, sometimes to the Racecourse or the Plantation near Ramsbury Manor. There was a cricket pitch there and lots of daisies. We spent hours making daisy chains which we put round our wrists and necks and in our hair.

Sometimes we collected wild flowers for the Annual Flower Show which was held on August Bank Holiday on Parliament Piece Meadow. That was quite a day for the villagers, the men showed vegetables and the women table decorations, cakes and jam. Our school did darning, embroidery and wild flowers. The flowers which we had collected, perhaps days before, were kept fresh in buckets of water in the pantry at home. The Flower show had coconut shies and other side shows. There were races; three legged races, egg and spoon and sack races. Prizes were a shilling for the first and sixpence for the second. If we won and had some money left we would buy something to take home for mother. Mother very rarely went out, sometimes to the bottom of the court to watch the carnival go by.

When I was about twelve years old a new family came to the village. That, in itself was quite an event, as most villages were very close communities. But the new family had a daughter, about my age, and we soon became friends. Her name was Pamela. We often went for long walks together; sometimes on a Sunday we would walk to Chilton Foliat to look at the church and we often stayed to the service in the evening. Pamela pressed wild flowers which we picked on our walks."

THE VILLAGE

"Ramsbury was supposed to be the biggest village in Wiltshire, whatever they mean by that, but it was really just two main streets, Oxford Street and High Street, and a few lanes. There wasn't much industry and most depended on farms and big houses for a living. My brother Sidney did many jobs and once worked for one of the grocers for a while when he left school and then he went to Ramsbury Manor to work in the gardens. I think that that was when Sir Frances and Lady Burdett lived there; after that he went keepering for Colonel Jones and then he went to the war.

The busiest place near Mount Pleasant was Bill Watts' blacksmiths shop at the bottom of Blind Lane. To us kids the place was a magnet. Bill Watts was quite a character! If I live to be a hundred I shall always see him in my mind's eye. He had a big bushy beard and the oldest and dirtiest leather apron you ever saw! He allowed children to take the bellows to the fire whenever he wanted to heat up the metal. There were two troughs at the bottom of the forge, one with small coal and the other with water. Very black water. He taught us how much of each to put on the fire and we watched in wonderment as he hammered the white-hot iron into shape on the anvil. Then, when he'd finished, plunging it into water to cool. There were always horses being shod and I can still see the sparks flying as he hammered the bars of steel into shoes, and recall the pungent smell of burning as the hot shoes were seated to make an impression on the hoof. High spots were cut away with a small sharp knife until a perfect fit was made, and then the shoes were nailed on, clenched and rasped. Sometimes, Bill Watts would throw a penny into the stinking black water of the bosh-tank, just for the pleasure of seeing us kids search for it with our sleeves rolled up. When he made iron tyres for the farm carts he would get us to help him pouring water on to the hot tyre as it was shrunk on to the wooden wheel with much steaming and hissing.

There were three or four grocer's shops in Ramsbury: Rosier's, Vokin's and Hill's in the High Street. We usually bought our groceries at the nearest. Some also sold paraffin and milk. Rosier's sold theirs at the back door. Sugar was weighed up in rough blue paper bags, rice and tapioca in brown ones and sweets in a twist of paper like a funnel. Both margarine and butter were cut from large blocks and patted into shape with wooden butterpats. Sid said where he worked it seemed that the poorest families could only afford the cheapest marge. But at Mount Pleasant we always had pre-wrapped Blue Band. How snobbish are the 'genteel' poor!

I always spent my 'Saturday-Penny' at Rosier's and it took me ages to make up my mind. A ha'penny worth of aniseed balls would last the longest if you only sucked them, but sometimes, we had liquorice in long, wide pieces which we tore into strips like leather boot laces. Sometimes Leonard Rosier would give me a sweet but not if his father was about!

At the end of the week when mother's money began to run out we would have to ask the grocer for credit, which meant there would often be an outstanding bill. It would mean, if we had ten shillings for shopping, two shillings would have to go towards the debt.

Sam Bull was the village chimney sweep who lived somewhere in Oxford Street. Meat was bought from Rumball's in The Square, usually two shillings or two shillings and sixpence for a really decent family joint. Meat for Sunday roast meant that dad had to saw more wood for the fire.

Milk was brought to the door in cans and measured into jugs. Eggs we usually got from Granny Giddings at number one, but if hers were off lay we would go to Talmadges at the bottom of the Lane opposite the Knapp. There we got thirteen eggs for a shilling which, with mashed potatoes, was enough for all of us for dinner.

Very rarely mother would buy some flowers. She would send us down to Miss White who lived at the Knapp. Miss White always took us into the garden with her while she picked the flowers and afterwards, would give us each an apple.

The main public house in Ramsbury was *The Bell* in The Square where there was also *The Windsor Castle*. Franklins kept *The Bell* and they also had a butcher's shop in the High Street. Most of the shops in The Square were owned by Tom Pullen who was an antiques and furniture dealer. He was very well-known and people used to come from miles around to his shop. The variety of articles he dealt in was fascinating and I used to spend hours just looking in his shop window.

Carter's were the ironmongers. They sold everything but the speed of service was not good and unless there was no one else in the shop you had to wait ages before getting served. There was never any 'sell-by' date on the packets in those days and the same stocks would appear on the counter year after year.

The landlord of *The Crown*, that is *The Crown and Anchor*, at the top of Blind Lane was Mr Burton. Beer was cheap but money was short. Dad never went there more than twice a week, mostly only once, and even then a glass would have to last him all the evening; it had to! If we kids went to *The Crown* for a bottle of lemonade we had to go to the back door. Lemonade bottles always had glass marbles in their necks but there was always a penny on the bottle if you took it back. So it didn't really pay to smash the bottle to get the marble, which some boys did. Marbles were plentiful and cheap and you could buy brown clay marbles and coloured glass marbles in most sweet shops.

The village had two bakers, Sheppard's in The Square and Vokin's in Oxford Street. In the summer, when we didn't have a fire at home, mother would send us with a bread pudding to the bakers to be cooked in their oven after they had baked the day's bread. This service cost a penny and quite a few of the villagers used this facility. We would stand and watch the baker take out the last loaves with a long wooden peel and, when the bread was out, in went the puddings!

The Post Office was kept by Mr Pinniger and I'm sure we had the same postman, Mr Clements, for as long as I can remember. In Back Lane, down by The Square, was Mr Treble, Bespoke Tailor; famous, far and wide, as a breeches maker. He made most of the breeches for the lads at the racing stables at Lambourn. It was at Trebles that Ciss Chandler, the keeper's daughter from Park, who later married my brother Sid, learned her trade.

The shoemakers were the Hunters, father and son, in Oxford Street. The repair service took weeks. We couldn't afford shoe menders so dad did most of the mending that was required, at least while we were all small. If ever we had a new pair of shoes or boots, which was very rare, half-moon protectors were put on both toes and heels. We were dared to play hop-scotch in new shoes and we always changed into an old pair to play outside in the evenings.

Charlie Sparrow, who lived in Oxford Street, was a pastry maker on a very small scale. He always had a few jam tarts in the window of his terrace house but he was better known for his poems and monologues. Even after eighty years my brother Gordon can still remember some and he's put a few of them on tape.

This is how the first one goes. It's called 'A Race for a Sweetheart'.

'Volks sez Oi be zilly, but why they should talk zo Oi can't understand. Oi tell'e Oi look quite a swell wi' a stick in me 'and. Oi don't get about loike the rest of young men, daily Oi vollow the plough. Oi bain't zuch a vule as zum volk may think Oi can tell a letter 'a' from a cow! That's more'n zum of 'em can do.

Oi don't fancy the scream in me 'eart, but Oi be near broken down ... zince my gals gone to town. Oi can't tell exactly zir why.. O, maybe 'ers met another bloke theer ... but smarter! Oi 'ope not, for Oi love 'er to me 'earts bottom place. To lose 'er, oh dear Oi should die. Oi got a job, zee zir, to win 'er thus far. Maybe thats what makes 'er more zweet. She's got zuch nice eyes, 'bout the zise o' mince pies ... an; zuch arms! An' talk about veet! Good Lard they be bigger'n moine! An' 'er sprawls about zo ... an' 'er walk, tis all up an down. An' 'er 'airs all loike wool .. a soft as you loike, an' 'er face never carries a frown.

This beautiful gal met Oi larst July when Oi were a roamin about, 'er spoke to Oi vust, Good Lard! Oi thought Oi should bust! You can't take 'ow that put me out! That is to zay it made me veel kind of narvous yer know, Oi've never velt queerer afore. But when Oi come round Oi thought it were good on 'er a squeezin' me 'and until it were zore.. Oh Bless 'e, Oi can put up wi' that zort o'thing ... If Oi can make 'er my wife she would bring joy! She's loike a child's toy, amusing, perplexing one's loife ... An' talk about zingin'! Why Bless yer zir, my zingin's awfully grand. Why theeser think Oi've never travelled about a bit Oi can never understand. She zings zo delightful, She were zingin' to Oi t'other night when we were a-strayin'.. Let's zee it were the night when we were zayin' as 'ow we couldn't leave one another, Anyway, we go part o' the way to my 'ome and then Oi'd go back agin wi' 'er. Arter a bit we got on 'er mother's doorstep. It was just a gettin' dark an' Oi 'ad my arm roun' 'er zweet waist, now an' then a givin' of 'er a smacker an' Oi 'eard zummat frizzin' inzide. An' Oi zes to 'er 'Molly' Oi zaid, 'Whats that?' An she zaid, 'It's mother fryin' sprats'.

Just then, all of a zudden loike 'er mother comes to the door an' 'er chucks that pan o' sprats clean over Oi! Zo Oi ran an' Molly ran, an' 'er father ran an' 'er mother ran. Oi tar down that strit loike Billy-O! Wi' all of 'em arter me! An' at larst Oi ran into an old woman, quoite accidental loike. She were a comin' out of a shop wi' a basket of eggs on 'er arm. Oi cut'er clean over! Oi never stopped to zee what 'er looked loike, but Molly 'ave told Oi zince as 'ow when they got 'er up an' got 'er back into that there shop, 'er were all yaller!

But 'er zingin'! Lard Bless yer, 'er can zing!

Now you listen, Oi'll try'n imitate 'er ...

(Sings in a falsetto voice)

Dear Sweetheart, come an' kiss me,

Give me one before you go,

Tell me that you'll sadly miss me,

As we wander to an' fro ...

Little Sweetheart come an' kiss me? An Bless 'e Oi'vr done that many a toime. But Zir, Oi 'ad to run for 'er once, up that there station, an' Oi can tell you Oi was zittin in an awkward situation. A feller what 'ad bin wi' she a longish toime afore, 'e was a-goin'to meet 'er too. Zo both of us a started to run to zee' 'oo would get there vust. An' Oi got there, look you, all out o' puff. Molly when she zeed t'other bloke, she began to cry, an'she zaid, 'What dust t'other bloke want 'ere? Oi never zent fir 'im!

An' then Oi thought Ou'd try an' frighten t'other bloke away. Zo Oi zets up me back zo fashioned an' 'Shoo! Shoo!' Oi went, but it frightened Molly instead of t'other bloke an' 'er vainted right off. An' when 'er come round 'er clung to t'other chap an' zaid as 'ow 'er wouldn't ave nuthin' to do wi' Oi 'er makin' zuch a big row.

But we made it up an' 'ers gone to a new place. She's zweeter by far, (Honest), She's zweeter than a tart, but Oi shall never forget the day Oi ran for my zweet'eart.'

So that's Charlie Sparrow for you! There was a different poem, or monologue every week. Another one that Gordon recited in his Ramsbury concert party days is about a chap named Potts who was very fond of a tipple. I don't think that he can remember the beginning but it goes on like this ...

'... and would come home quite fresh. As fresh as new paint!

If she said, "Potts! You're drunk!" He'd say, "Hic! No I aint!"

One night he came home very late from his club,

They'd been giving those ignorant MP's a rub.

The church clock struck one as he opened the door,

He climbed up the stairs to the second floor

And listened a moment! - "Asleep! That's her snore!"

He crept in the room on the tips of his toes

So as not to disturb his good lady's repose

He took off his coat and his hat, very slow,
Tried to wind up his watch, but it wouldn't go.
And feeling so thirsty, he looked round to find
A drop of cold water! And there! Just to his mind,
A goblet! Filled ready! He said, "Thish ish kind!
She know I'd be thirsty!" - He seized it with glee
Determined the bottom he'd very soon see.
He took a long pull, - and then! Oh dear me!
He gulped, - almost choked! Dropped the glass on the floor
Where it smashed into atoms! With an effort he tore
Something out of his mouth, and it rolled to the floor.
Then, at the risk of alarming the house,
He shouted, "I've almost swallowed a mouse!"'
And he took up a water jug to give it a douse!
Now Mrs Potts had woken up in a terrible fright.
She made for the gas, and turned up the light
Then she saw her husband in a terrible plight.
He had his foot upon something. He shouted,
"Bring a poker! Bring anything! Bring a thick stick!
I'll keep my foot down while you strike at it! Quick!"
Mrs Potts, like most women, a tiger might meet,
Or a drove of wild bullocks, might pass in the street,
But a mouse! Oh! a mouse was too much of a treat!
So, she took up the poker and aimed for its head
But caught Potts a blow on his best corn instead!
And asked, in a quivering voice, "Is it dead?"
Then said Potts, in a range, "Give the poker to me!
I'll settle this hash immediately!"
So, he took up the poker and aimed for its head,
"That's killed him!" he said, "and, says I "Sarves him right!"
Mrs Potts had bent down with the candle alight,

Then she drew herself up like a queen and she said,

"You silly old idiot! Get off to bed!

I always thought that you were wrong in your head!

You've soaked your poor brains until they're nothing but blubber!

That's not a mouse Sir! That's India Rubber!

That's the top of the baby's bottle you lubber!"

Another of Gordon's incomplete local poems runs ...

A woodman with his donkey stopped outside a barber's shop.

The barber said, "What will you take for all your little lot?"

The woodcutter had travelled far and had sold but little stock

So no wonder that the question gave him a sudden shock.

But, when he had regained his breath, he answered with a crack,

I'll take sixpence for all the wood upon the donkey's back!"

"Just put it down beneath that broken shed," the barber said.

The woodman did as he was told, then led his ass away,

The barber came to his shop door and shrieked!

"Come back! Come back I say!

The bargain was for all the wood.

The panniers are wood and I must have them too!

You don't deny that? What! Not justice? The Law decides!"

Then said the woodman, "You take me for a fuel!"' .....

And there memory gets the upper hand! Of course the last word should be 'fool', but I've heard Gordon say 'fuel' by mistake and it brings the house down!

But to get back to Ramsbury. It might have been called a village but it did have a Town Crier! When we were kids it was Mr Frank Rushden. He would walk round the village ringing his bell and every so often he would stop and shout out his announcement. We kids never listened to what he said, we'd just crowd round him calling 'Oyez! Oyez!'

Finally the pubs. There were more than enough. On the other hand there was no telly and no wireless and no cinema until they started having a film once a week in the village hall. So pubs it had to be! As well as *The Crown*, *The Bell* and *The Windsor Castle* there was also *The Halfway* at the Whittonditch end, *The Burdett* and *The Malt Shovel* down the High Street and *The Bleeding Horse* at the West End. And that's not all! Down the bottom was *The Boot*. This was a pub that hadn't changed since the day it was built. Stone floors, scrubbed deal tables and forms and a heavy thatch overhanging the road. Of course they couldn't all last, *The Halfway*, *The Boot*, *The Windsor Castle* and *The Bleeding Horse* have all closed ... That's progress!

VILLAGE SCHOOLDAYS

"I started my education at the mixed infant school in Back Lane. My only recollections of that period are of very small chairs and the daily ritual of 'Good Morning, Miss Nicklin' when we arrived in class, and 'Goodnight, Miss Nicklin' when we went home. If we misbehaved we were made to stand up in front of the class. When Miss Nicklin got annoyed she would pull our hair.

I did not like infant school.

When I was seven years old I moved across the road to the 'big' school - the girls' Church of England. There we had good teachers and it was there that I came to love reading and composition. Arithmetic was my poorest subject and I had many more crosses than ticks in my exercise book. I could only just about manage long division, and that was about all.

There were three teachers, Miss Madge took classes one and two, Miss Prismall classes three and four, and the Headmistress took classes five, six and seven. We didn't call them 'classes' in those days, we knew them as 'standards'.

Miss Greenway was an excellent teacher. Her favourite subject was needlework. We were taught to 'run and fell', 'French seam', 'chain stitch', 'feather stitch', 'smock', as well as embroidery, darning and knitting. They tell me that schools no longer teach knitting ... why ever not? I suppose its the knitting machines they've got nowadays.

When Miss Greenway left, Miss Gardner took her place. In the spring and summer we were taken for long 'nature rambles' to gather wild flowers, grasses and leaves. The next day, in class, we were told to draw some of the specimens and they would also be used for nature study.

Like most children I could be naughty sometimes. One day, when I had been particularly naughty, I was made to stand in the corner with my hands on my head. I soon got tired of this and started to make signs to the other children with my fingers. The girls began to giggle so Miss Greenway slapped me with a ruler and shut me in the 'little room'. This was a closet where they kept all the new exercise books, pencils and rubbers, and a large wicker basket with the dressing-up clothes for the school plays. So I was able to have a good rummage round.

At twelve o'clock, dinner-time, Miss Greenway turned the key in the lock! I was a prisoner! To this day I think that this was an extra punishment I didn't deserve! What else could it have been? Anyway the other children went home to dinner and I was left alone! As time went by I began to feel sorry for myself and by the time the children came back to school I was crying. I don't think that I was really bothered when Miss Greenway let me out, but, for her, a sobbing child must have been the last straw. So she sent me home.

When I got home mother asked me why I had not come home to dinner and when I told her what had happened she gave me a good ticking off as well! It wasn't a good day! But school days weren't all dismal. In Springtime we would dance around the Maypole with Miss Prismall chanting, 'Blues under ... Reds over ... Whites in the outer ring ...', and really that dancing was a school highlight.

Then there was the school Treat. Mr Oakes, an elderly gentleman who lived at 'The Cedars' paid for it. He hired a large open charabanc from Mr Reeves to take all the older girls to Bournemouth for the day.

The evening before the outing, three of us, Dora and Mary Westall, who were cousins to each other, and myself, knelt down in their woodshed and prayed for a fine day. Our faith and our prayers were answered and the sun shone brilliantly. It was my first trip to the seaside and, of course, my very first sight of the sea. In the summer, especially during the school holidays, we played all sorts of games. Hop-Scotch, Rounders, Tag, Hide-and-Seek and Cricket. We played mostly in the Lane although there was plenty of grassy fields around where we could have gone. We spent a lot of time in the hay and corn fields which were then filled with the gentle chatter of horse-drawn mowers and binders. Sometimes we took bottles of lemonade made from Eiffel Tower Lemonade Crystals. We had wads of bread and cheese, and sat down under a tree for a picnic with the men while the sweaty horses munched the chop in their nosebags. There were no balers then and all the hay had to be loaded by hand on to wagons and drawn to a stack in the corner of the field.

At corn harvest we would help shock-up the heavy sheaves which were often wet with dew and thick with prickly thistles. The sharp stubble scratched our bare legs and, by the end of the day, they would be quite red and sore. When the binder, drawn by two horses, had only a small uncut patch of corn left standing in the middle of the field, everyone would space themselves out round the field to force those rabbits remaining, back into the uncut corn, back into an ever smaller patch. Some people had dogs and these would stand on their hind legs to see over the sheaves lying on the ground, for a sight of any rabbit brave enough to make a break for it. Everyone had sticks and not many rabbits got away. I suppose it was cruel really, but there were so many rabbits everywhere in those days that they were a pest. What's more, everyone liked rabbit pie and going home with one for the pot, was like going home from a safari with a lion! When the corn was ready to cart, which might be some weeks, we led the horses drawing the wagons between the rows of stooks while the men, one or two on either side of the waggon pitched up sheaves to the man on top who built the load. Sometimes, if we were lucky, we would ride with the loader, but the heavy sheaves coming up from both sides would knock us off our feet. It was a bit easier at the stack. The rick-builder was a very skilled man who was very particular how each sheaf was laid. He would work kneeling down with knee-pads of sacking tied to his legs with binder twine. He'd work round and round the stack laying each sheaf carefully, the right way up and each row overlapped like roof-tiles to keep the rain out and the unthreshed ears of corn dry. Any loose corn dropped from the sheaves or binder was left in the field for the gleaners. That is, anyone from the village who had a few cooby-chicks down their gardens. Both my brothers caught rabbits. I suppose it helped with their pocket money, not to mention mother's housekeeping. Practically all the older boys and young men went poaching in those days.

There were always lots of games played in the village square. The big hollow tree that stood in the middle was a good hiding place and gave rise to all sorts of pranks. If we wanted to go further afield we had to walk. There were few bicycles about but it was possible to hire one from Mr Coster in the High Street for threepence an hour. The bikes were pretty ramshackle and they often broke down, and the very gritty roads caused lots of punctures. When we could afford it we used to ride to Hungerford or Marlborough which was quite a change from a long, long walk. Of course, that was long before the last war when we used to go to Marlborough Mop. That was the fair they used to have in the main street.

In those days it was walking that gave me most pleasure. Walking in pursuit of nature made it seem so different. Picking king-cups in the water-meadows, mushrooming, blackberrying or even fishing for tiddlers and in the autumn there were hazel-nuts. My father used to say that the nuts were not ready until you could shake them down from the trees.

In fact my brother remembers that dad used to sing a song that went ... 'The nuts are high, they are so brown, The nuts are high, they might come down ...'

But that's about all he can remember now. Of course if you pick nuts before they are ripe they only shrivel. When we took nuts home Dad would put them in a big brown stone jar and cover them with salt. Kept that way they'd last until Christmas. Well, some of them. By the time Christmas came there was always some short ... taken by 'nobody'.

Wooding was more than a problem, it was really on all the year round, because everyone relied on wood for cooking and heating the house. You couldn't afford to buy expensive coal when there was wood lying around rotting. There was a spinney called Whitehill within a couple of miles and that was our favourite place. Usually I'd go with Maud Skerry from next door and Liza Rose from number six. It was they who taught me which wood to choose, that which burnt best, and how to tie the faggots with a bit of binder twine. If a faggot was not properly tied it would fall apart on the way home and have to be retied. Maud always took a saw in case there was a big limb blown down in the wind. But we always had to be careful about the noise the saw made and so one of us always had to keep a sharp look-out for the keeper."

BIG HOUSES, POSH PEOPLE, PARTIES AND PICNICS

"The gentry in big houses are rarely part of village life except, perhaps, for high-days and holidays. The Manor, Littlecote, the Round House and Hilldrop were mostly just names. Sometimes their goings-on made a splash and I can remember just such an occasion when the daughter of the Woodlands, who lived at Marridge Hill, got married at Ramsbury Church. The Woodlands owned a store in Knightsbridge in London, and they put on a real do! The whole village turned out! It was a real Society wedding. We'd never seen anything like it! They even had the Huntsmen with their red coats and all the hounds waiting at the lych gate for the couple to emerge from the church.

One Christmas, Frederick Giddins at Crowood put on a party for the children. He had a large Christmas Tree put up in the hall and it nearly touched the ceiling! We had plenty to eat and each of the fifty boys and girls was given a present wrapped in fancy paper. At the end we all walked home to the village in the pitch-black night.

Parties were for the posh. Ordinary people couldn't afford them. I can only remember one birthday party. That was for Mary Watts. Her father was a farmer and horse dealer. They cleaned out the barn at the bottom of the Lane and put up trestle-tables. I can't remember what we had to eat but we were all given one of those paper ticklers that shoot out when you blow it.

There were no picnics as there are today, just the lemonade and bread and cheese ones that I've told you about, in the hay and corn fields. But sometimes we'd have a special picnic at the top of Spring Hill just where it was covered with clover and that little yellow flowered Tom Thumb. From there you could see the whole of the village laid out before you. It was a good place to play roly-poly, which meant rolling down the hill-side into the bushes.

Treats were few and far between. Sometimes we had honey in the comb from the poultry farm at Whittonditch. In the winter we all went to the Band of Hope or the Girls' Friendly Society. There we did sewing while somebody read a suitable book. At home we had a wind-up gramophone with a record that had 'Blaze Away' on one side and 'Under the Double-eagle' on the other. Wireless sets were for the rich, but mum always sang a lot and Olive remembers some of the songs, and here are snatches she's written down. The first one is about food ... probably Vokin's Suet Pudding!

'Pudden, Pudden, gie Oi lots o'pudden
Gi'e Oi any kind o'duff
Plain or spotted, that's the stuff, Oi don't care what kind it is,
As long as its a good 'un,
For when I'm old Oi can use my gums
For there ain't no bones in pudden!"

It sounds a bit 'music hall' to me! Then there was Rickaticatic!
'My wife she's gone to the fair,
An I think she must be spendin',

While I poor soul sits 'ere
An' these old shoes are mendin',
With a ric-a-tic-a-tic-a-tic,
With a ric-a-tic a tearo!
With a ric-a-tic-a-tic-a-tic,
Because she is my dearo!

I've lost my ball of wax,
Now isn't that provoking?
I've found a little bit,
Now I can go on working.
With a ric-a-tic-a-tic-a-tic,
With a ric-a-tic a tearo!
With a ric-a-tic-a-tic-a-tic,
Because she is my dearo!'

Then Olive remembers a verse, probably about Queen Victoria.

'Oi tell 'e Garge, what Oi did zee, When Oi did go to Lunnon Town,
Oi zeed 'er gercious Majesty,
A wearin' on a golden crown.
Lawks a mussy me Garge
They don't do that shur-ly
The things they do, they do do,
Well, they do, do, so do Oi!'

Somewhere in that song it mentions the Queen being in a carriage.

'Wi' a pair o' greys An' a coach so gay, An' a scotch chap zittin' up behind!'

And then there's Gordon's special.

'She's fourteen stone,
An' every bit 'er own,
An' the colour on 'er cheeks ain't paint,
She's forty round the calf, When Brown began to laugh,
For my love takes the cake.
An' up Oi came wi' my little lot,
Zaid Oi, this can't be whacked,
She fell off the moke,
An' 'er funny bone was broke,
An' 'er boko was a little bit stretched ...
'She's fourteen stone,
An' every bit 'er own,
An' the colour on 'er cheeks ain't paint,
She's forty round the calf,
When Brown began to laugh,
For my love takes the cake ...'

I wonder who Brown was supposed to be?

I can't remember whether dad ever sang that one but I can remember him coming home every Saturday night after he'd been for his pint. He'd come down the Lane and grab the latch of the door, then come in and say, 'Ere I am gal, safe and sound!' And mum used to reply, 'You look like it!' Sometimes during the week, he might run out of tobacco and he'd offer about, doing little things. If he wasn't able to earn much mum would sense something was wrong and she'd say, 'All right Harry, what's the matter? Havn't you got any tobacco?' And he'd say, 'No mother, 'alf an ounce'll do'. And then I'd go up to Rosier's and get an half ounce of Red Bell."

SUNDAYS

"Sunday was a special day because on Sunday we always wore our best clothes. You could say that we had clothes for Sunday only. Father was very strict about Sunday and there was a lot of things we were not allowed to do on the Lord's Day. Cutting finger nails was one. Cleaning shoes was another. Shoes for Sunday had to be cleaned on Saturday. I remember one Sunday when Hilda had forgotten to clean her shoes. Father was out somewhere and so she decided to risk it. When she had cleaned one shoe father came in.

'What's this, my lady?' he asked sharply. (He always called us girls 'my lady' when he was cross with us) ... Of course Hilda had to stop immediately and she was sent off to Sunday School with one clean and one dirty shoe. She tried to clean the dirty shoe on the way but no amount of spitting on hankies and rubbing made any difference.

The reward for attending Sunday School was a religious stamp which we stuck into special books. You were supposed to collect a set; there was lots of swopping and it took ages and ages to fill a book, but perhaps that was what it was all about!

Sometimes we were allowed to go to the proper Church Service after Sunday School but the vicar must have decided that he couldn't deliver his sermon with a lot of children fidgeting about so, after hymns and prayers, we were usually marched out!

In nice weather we often went for a walk after we left church and in the spring we'd go up Crowood Lane which was a good place for primroses and violets. Mother loved violets and father often took her some home carefully laid in the fold of his cap. She arranged them in egg cups and lined them up on the window sill. In the last years of her life she was so crippled with arthritis she had to have her bed downstairs by the window and these violets and other flowers gave her great pleasure.

A few weeks before father died he too had to have his bed downstairs in the opposite corner of the room. I suppose they were company for each other but it was very sad.

On Sunday evenings in the winter, we would sit round the fire and sing hymns. Dozens of them. Hilda and my brothers had good singing voices but I was tone deaf! Mother kept all of them together, but not me!

My parents were Primitive Methodists, and when we were very young we went to chapel. To the Congregational in the High Street. The teacher was Miss Harrison. The Harrisons owned the draper's shop in the village.

Once a year the Chapel celebrated its Anniversary. For this event we all learnt long recitations. Mother was very patient and taught each of us an appropriate poem or monologue. The one I remember best was called 'Lead us not into Temptation' but it's so long ago that I can't quite recall all of it, but I'll do my best.

'A pale-faced boy with quivering lips, stood in the prison dock,
There was no sound in the crowded room save the tick, tick, tick of the clock
His widowed mother stood beside his tiny sister there,
Her thin, pale lips were moving slow, as if in silent prayer.
Her husband had lived an honest life, upright, straightforward, true,
But now his son stood in the dock, she knew not what to do.
The prosecutor, stern and hard, stood frowning at the boy,
Then smiled a bitter, cruel smile, of fierce malignant joy,
With eager haste he told his tale, he had engaged the lad,
To run errands, and never thought he would turn out so bad.
One day, he missed a shilling, and judge what bitter grief,
He found his honest errand boy was nothing but a thief.
Such was his tale, told in a tone of mingled spite and rage,
Without one sympathetic word for the poor lad's tender age.
And then the Counsel rose to speak, it was his maiden brief,
A kind young man whose heart was touched by the poor widow's grief.
He turned to where the huge law books lay, ranged there with legal pride
But 'twas not for these he sought, he took a surer guide.
He took up the New Testament, the lawyers smiled to see,
But one look at his eager face, cut short their ill-timed glee.
He turned the pages o'er and read, while all sat silent there,
'Leads us not into Temptation' from The Lord's Prayer.
And then he told how this mean man had tempted the poor lad,
And placed the money in his sight; enough to drive him mad.
How he had placed it 'neath the mat where the lad would have to sweep,
Then cautiously as any cat would round the corner creep.
How the poor lad at last gave way, his mother wanted bread,
He took the shilling, bought the loaf, he had found the coin he said.
It was the truth, he had found it where it never should have been
Placed there to lead the lad astray by a master cruel and mean.
The Counsel ceased, - the jury then acquitted the poor boy,
Again the widow's tears o'er flowed, but they were tears of joy.
And the young lawyer, then unknown, his first case made his name,
And soon with persevering toil he rose to wealth and fame.
And so we pray, 'Preserve us all from Famine, Fire and Sword,'
And, add this Petition, 'Lead us not into Temptation Lord.'

And that's it! I can't remember it all and I expect when I first learnt it, it rhymed! But it's very Victorian. A poem with a moral and suitable for a Great Day.

The most important thing for our Sunday School Anniversary was that we all had new dresses. Hilda made the dresses. She was very good. We would walk five miles to Hungerford, to Bodman's shop up the end of the town, to get the material. This was because it was cheaper there than anywhere else; about sixpence three farthings a yard. Miss Boniface, a real 'bonny-face', was the assistant at Bodmans and she usually sold us Miss Moffit prints. We always bought enough material for matching dresses ... it was more economical that way. But we each had a different colour ribbon sash to tone with the colours of the print. The new straw hats we bought from Harrisons in the village and trimmed them with ribbons and artificial forget-me-nots, or perhaps cherries. When we put them on I really preened in front of the mirror!

When Anniversary was over the hats and ribbons were put carefully away in a wooden box in the front bedroom. We had no wardrobe and all the clothes were folded and kept in boxes or a chest of drawers.

Gordon and Sid used to go to Bible Classes on Sunday afternoons at Miss Meyricks at Ridgelands, on the Whittonditch road.

That was religion and Sundays in Ramsbury then, but to me now, religion and Ramsbury means the Church. It's a beautiful old church, both Sid and Gordon used to sing in the choir long, long ago, and now ... Mum and Dad lie buried in the churchyard."

CONVERSATIONS

SID'S STORY

"Of course you can't write it all down, but our Gladys has done very well to do what she had, but there's still a lot more.

Like when I was fourteen I worked for Sid Watts for a while. Now, he was a horse dealer, and he used to go down to Wales and buy all these sucking colts, just away from their mothers. And we had to drive them from the other side of Ogbourne over the downs to Marlborough. That was when the sheep fair was up on the Common in them days. Of course we used to ride ponies and drive them, but we went all over Wiltshire with horses, many a week at a time. Sid Watts would have these colts up there, see, and sell a few, go to Devizes and he would sell some of them and maybe he would keep one or two. Of course they weren't all sucking colts, some we used to call Bovril horses. They was a pound a leg then! They was knacker's horses. They were finished, see?

I've took as many as six, remember I was only about fourteen then, and we used to take them to Lambourn, and meet up with another feller who would take them off me. It was Brook Alder from Wantage, and he'd take them on. I've known this feller get on a horse and the horse drop dead underneath him. I used to take six at a time but I might not get more than four there. They was on their last legs! They weren't dying see, but they was walking towards the knackers. They weren't ill-treated or nothing, but some didn't get there. If one dropped dead, that was nothing. Like there was a woman who dropped dead in Fine Fare the other day, and she was only a young woman!"

"Can you remember much about working at the grocers and in the Manor Gardens?" asked Gladys.

"That I can," said Sid, "When I first started gardenin' I worked with an' old jobbin' gardener. The best gardener I've ever known! Jacob Rushes was his name, an' he could tell a tale! He used to say to me, 'Do you know a certain shopkeeper in the village?' an' I'd say 'Yes', an' he'd say 'Well he's got a boy workin' for him, an' every mornin' he says to this boy, 'have you damped the tobacco boy?' 'Yes, Sir.' 'An' have you sanded the sugar, boy?' 'Yes, Sir', and then th'old shopkeeper 'ud say, 'Good boy, come in to Prayers!' But times were hard then an' even the shopkeepers had a job to make ends meet."

"I don't know about 'make ends meet'" said Gordon, "When Dad was on the dole, mother used to have to watch every penny. Some of the shopkeepers were the biggest twisters out. Why they'd sell what they called 'Best Bacon' but it was really a bit of old sow with the tits on!"

"That's right!" said Gladys, "One of them used to put his finger on the scales! He used to weigh his finger! My Mum used to say 'Watch him!' didn't she? ... You know those old fashioned blue bags? Well he'd shovel sugar, or rice or somethin' into it an' he'd put it on the scales an' he'd press! One day I said to him, cause I was only little then, 'You're pressin' that bag down!' an' he said, 'I'm not!' an' I said, 'You are ... my mum said I had to watch you!'"

Sid laughed, and went on, "Another thing they used to do was hold the bag up high an' drop it down so that it'd weigh quicker, or p'raps with the bag on the scales pour the stuff in from high up, like when some people have just made a pot o' tea, hold the teapot up high, then when the tea's weaker, hold it closer to the cup!"

"Do you remember our Dad saying 'Water betwitched an' tea begrudged!'" said Gordon, "He used to say husband's tea an' she used to say 'Its bloomin' good tea!'"

Gordon went on, "Dad was a fine man, though he wasn't born in Ramsbury, he was born at Oare, over Pewsey, an' mother came from Richmond in Surrey."

"That's right," said Sid, "Dad came as blacksmith at the Foundry, 'twas Osmond's. There was three smiths' shops in Rambury then..."

Gordon interrupts. "There was more than three ... There was Bill Watts ..."

"With the big beard," said Sid, "an' Pope, an' Johny Winchcombe, ... now tell me t'other one ...?"

"There was Charlie Winchcombe," Gordon corrected the name, at *The Bleedin' Horse*, Pope up Crowood Lane, Bill Watts at the bottom of Blind Lane ..."

"An' the Foundry ..." Sid agrees.

"I used to go down nights, when I was quite a kid, an' strike for 'ol Bill Watts," Gordon paused then went on with pride, "He said he'd rather have me strike for him than one o' the men."

Gordon paused again. "'Cause then I was cheaper!"

"I used to help too, when I was old enough," said Sid "I used to take the shoes off the hosses, an' when he'd put the clip on, turn the nails over, file the hoofs an' get out the ol' pot of oil an' oil the hoofs ... It cost about four bob to shoe a horse all round then. Its about eighteen quid now!"

Sid continued. "Our dad was a Master Blacksmith an' Farrier. When he was a boy I think he used to work for Pope's at Ma'lborough an' he walked all the way from Oare! Twice a day! An' very often there were horses to be shod early on! I could never quite make out how we were related to the Popes but dad said we were, an' Tommy Pope once told me that he had a chest at home that once belonged to my grandmother Eliza. That were the Tommy Pope who was once Mayor of Ma'lborough. We must have been related because I can remember Tommy Pope coming down to the Recreation Ground in Salisbury Road, when we lived there after the war an' he used to show me letters and photographs he'd been sent from Jessie, dad's sister, who'd gone to Australia with her family years before. But dad really learned his trade an' I can remember reading this government paper saying that as a blacksmith he wouldn't be called up. That was in the Great War."

"Twas during the first war," said Gordon, "they used to make water barrels for France. They used to put me inside, when I was a kid, to paint them. Through a little square hole at the top. But Osmonds was a proper foundry. Dad used to make castings an' mouldin's, ... dad could do it all ... he were a clever bloke, no kiddin'".

"Ev'rybody in the village used to say 'Give Harry Hiscock a bit of iron an' he'll make anythin'," Sid paused, then he went on, "remember how they had him alter the eagle from the church? We had it up home ... They had the Reverend Wellesley, then Shuttleworth came, an' he was shorter, so it had to come down ..."

"Funny thing was," said Gordon, "Dad warn't ever so big, not for a blacksmith ..."

"Not like we three," said Gladys, "Mind my boys, John, Gerald an' Richard are like me ... in fact we're all well built, this generation. Must be the food ... they weren't so well fed, them days ..."

"As a kid," said Gordon, "I was only a little whippersnapper, not like now, but Dad was never big ..."

"Dad never put on an ounce in his life," said Sid.

"Fancy how he used to get up a five, walk to the Foundry", Gladys mused, "then he'd be back home at eight for breakfast havin' shod several horses. He worked hard, he used his brain. Even when you were grown up Gordon, when Winchcombe was schoolmaster, I remember 'ol Theo Wootton said to me, 'You know, Gladys, your dad was born thirty years too soon!' he had a fantastic brain, he really did. 'an Mum were the same. She stood out in the village didn't she?"

"The best writer I've ever seen," said Sid, "best hand writer, that is ... nobody could touch her for writin' ... 'an doin' crosswords. I've inherited it from her I suppose ... The first thing I do in the mornin' is to go to the loo, an' do the crossword. An' that's my day really ..."

"But if anyone used to come," said Gladys, "she'd always help. She must have been ever so patient, she used to write everybody's letters."

"Beautiful writin'" said Sid.

"Oh, marvellous," Gordon agreed, "We got some letters at 'ome now that she wrote..."

"Cause she was born at Richmond." Gladys thought for a while, "Richmond, Surrey," she went on, "Do you remember she always used to say that the boys at school used to call after her, 'Leonora Hobbs, Richmond Surrey, Cocked up her leg an' piddled in a 'urry!"

"But she didn't talk like us," said Gordon, "She warn't as crude as what we were. Not the way we talked, she was a different class altogether."

"She was good with us," said Gladys, "she'd try an' make us talk properly. Things like sound our "t's". We always had to say water, not waher."

"But there were all sorts o' words we used then," said Sid, "that seem to have gone. I mean we always kep' out vittles in a tommy box an' now its sandwiches in a lunch bag."

"An' I remember when we was very cold," Gordon interrupted, "We always said we were 'shrammed', that's right 'shrammed to death' we used to say. Then there's that word 'plimmed' ..."

"Well my daughter-in-law, Shirley," said Gladys, "I once said to her when we were doin' somethin', cookin' I mean, I said to her, 'I should leave it to 'plim. An' she didn't know what I mean't!"

"And there's another word Gladys," said Gordon, "I said to somebody once about 'daps' ..."

"Gymshoes" said Gladys.

"Plimsolls", reminded Gordon.

"Sid interrupted, "You remember when old Jim was in the police? Well he was sent up north to Nottingham or somewhere on a course an' the Sergeant shouted out, 'Right! Five minutes to get your plimsolls on!' an' course Jim didn't know what the hell he mean't! So he turned to another copper on the course, who came from Somerset, and' said, 'here, wot do he mean, bloody plimsolls?' Course the Somerset feller know, an' he turned to Jim an' said, 'He said, get yer daps on!'

Well, then Jim wus alright!"

"There's some funny local words everywhere, I suppose," said Gordon, "I mean some people are real broad Wiltshire ... What did we used to say if we wanted someone, say a child, to stay still somewhere...?"

"Bide 'yere" said Gladys, "never anythin' else ... but then if there was someone you didn't like we always said, 'I can't abide hem'".

"Then there's that old Wiltshire sayin'", said Gordon "Thee's a zilly, bisn't thee shit thee britches? Then thee comes an' went an' disn't ..." There his memory failed him.

Sid interrupted, "Go on!" he said, "There's more yet. "Zilly bisn't? Come from wesson disn't? Shit thee britches asn't? Casn't see'st 'swell as cust cast?"

"That's almost swearing," said Gladys, "Our Dad never swore though ... well, I only ever heard him swear once, an' that was when he was mendin' someone's shoes!"

"That's right," said Sid, "When I used to 'old the candle for him so's he could see to mend someone's kettle or somethin', he used to grunt an' go 'OOOh! Ah!. But he did swear sometimes, but it took a lot!"

Sid stopped to think and then went on, "Dad used to come up an' open out our rides when I was a-keeperin', an' that was a rough old job that'd make anyone swear. We used to give him the job in the summer, right up at Squirrel's Corner! About four an' half miles from Ramsbury! When I used to go round feedin' the pheasants he'd be there an' he'd say, 'I was sittin' here havin' a pipe at six o'clock this morning!' An' he'd walked four miles! An' he was sixty-seven or eight then! All them toffs who used to go shootin' at Colonel Jones' in them days thought the world of him. They used to walk along with their arms around his shoulders an' call him Harry! They'd make a hell of a fuss of him!"

"Four miles at that time of the mornin's a long way," said Gordon "'specially uphill, an' with heavy boots with hob nails! 'cause everyone wore hob nails with tips as well ... mind how dad used to make tips in the fire?"

"Talkin' about tips," said Sid, "I can remember one Boxin' Day I was up at Hen's Wood feedin' the birds. I had on a pair of these Bedford cords that do up in front, an' I had a loose tip on me boot. Well, someone came an' said that mother had fallen down an' broke her ankle, so I went down home an' got her to hospital. They put her down in one of the wards an' I had to walk there on a parquet floor! An' there was this loose tip a-goin' tip-tip all the time from me boot! Of course mother was insured, at that time if you took the News of the World, you was automatically insured for accidents in the home. Mind, they didn't want to pay an' I had a hell of a fight wi' them over it! I drew diagrams ... 'cause she'd tripped on the doorstep an' was half in an' half out! An' they said that she had to be inside the house. So as she was half in an' half out. In the end, we settled for half. But we had a hell of a fight!"

"That would be long after Dad finished at Osmond's I suppose," said Gordon, "he was there over thirty years an' sometime after the Wilsons took over the business they come to him one day an' told him he was too old! An' as a blacksmith there was no one to touch him! Like all blacksmiths in them days he made his own tools. Everything! Never bought a spanner, did he?"

"No," said Sid, "an' when he made them, he always made them on a crank like that, see?" (Sid demonstrates with his hands), "That way you had twice as much leverage! An' not only that, but you could get such a spanner into places where you couldn't get a straight 'un."

He paused, "Our dad was more'n a blacksmith. He used to drive the old traction engines as well! He knew every nut an' bolt! Why we had all those books at home! Big ones! Some weighin' a quarter of an' hundredweight! All wi' glossy pages! Do you know, he was the only man who could take a traction engine wi' a thresher an' baler behind down Elmdown Hill ... an' what'd that be Gordon, 'bout one in six?"

"I reckon," said Gordon, "but Dad, whether engine man or farrier, or blacksmith, was unbeatable. No job was too big or too small ... from tin kettles to traction engines, Harry Hiscock was the man! He was clever though, why I told a bloke the other day that my dad used to make chisels out of files an' rasps, an' this bloke said 't'weren't possible. He said they'd a flew! An' I said they didn't 'cause dad always put them in the fire."

"That's right," said Sid, "He'd get them just like that, an' dip them in the water, an' when they was that perfect blue colour, well, that was when they was hardened. But they didn't break. If you had an hard chisel an' hit him like that, he'd snap off at the end. They knew the colour. There was something in it! Ole Bill Watts was the same, wan't he? They used to 'old them up like that an' see them turnin' blue, an when they got to a certain difference they'd go 'Whop' into the bosh like that!"

"Ah!" said Gordon, "There's no blacksmiths like that anymore!"

"Everything's changed," said Sid, "I suppose most of the folk we knew when we was kids have gone. I was thinkin' ... do you remember just at the top of Blind Lane lived somebody called Pain? He was a roadman. An' just opposite was a woman called Mrs Duck. Well one day he was walkin' down the street an' he met Mrs Duck an' she said 'How are yer?' an' he said, 'Not too good, I've got a few pains,'an' she said, 'There'll be no pains in heaven!' an' he said 'There'll be no bloody ducks either!'"

Gladys said, "I remember Mrs Duck! She was only a little woman with short legs an' when she went to Rosier's she used to have to run to get there!"

"Do you remember Archibald Roberts?" asked Sid, "He came from a poor family at Marridge Hill. He used to have these great big old Army breeches an' puttees. They used to come to school like that an' when that old Army stuff got wet it did hum a bit! Well, one day, the boy sittin' next to him, 'twas Wilf Chamberlain, got up, an' the teacher said, 'Well, what is it?' An' Wilf Chamberlain said, 'Please Sir, Archibald stinks!'"

Gordon interrupted, "Yes, but those poor kids used to walk three miles to Ramsbury, sometimes in the dead of winter when it was rainin' an' by the time they got to school they'd be soaked to the skin. An' they sat in it all day long until half past three or four o'clock! Must have been terrible! An' then they 'ad to walk all that way home again. No wonder they smelt a bit!"

"Then there was Billy Bodfish," said Sid, "now that's an uncommon name! An' they walked four miles to school from Membury Lodge! Then there was the nicknames that folks had. Up where we lived there was Bind-head, an' Charlie Locke who we called Shimball next door ... Hobbs, now he didn't have a nickname at all did he? Did we used to call him 'Shaker' or somethin? an' then there was 'Pilate'."

"Remember Charlie Sparrow?" asked Gordon, "'E used to write poems an' things an' stick them up in his window with the cakes."

"That's right," said Sid, "when we was kids he used to invite the lads round. Although he used to make these little pastries, I mean for a village, he was a little gentleman. Anyway we used to go round there an' have some of his cherry-topped cakes. An' he used to get these games on see, an' one of these games was to sit on a jam jar, an' cock one foot on top of another, so". He stretches out his legs and rests the heel of his right foot on the toe of his left. He wobbles his feet a little to demonstrate the instability of the position.

He continues, "On the floor on yer left hand side you had a box of matches an', on your right hand side you had a candle. All you had to do was to pick up the matches an' light the candle. Zounds easy 'nough, but 'tis suprisin' just 'ow difficult such a simple thing can be especially when you've had two cups o' strong coffee!"

"He used to get us boys at it! We was only kids really, but it was fun," said Gordon.

"There was another thing," said Sid, "We used to go down to the water-meadows at Whittonditch ... the shepherd had sheep down there with corncrakes. An' this shepherd said, 'When the birds go CARK! then you can walk towards them and they won't see or hear you but as soon as they stop, you got to stop.'"

"We had to try an' catch them," said Gordon, "This old shepherd told us that nobody could do it. The trick was supposed to be that you could move when they were croakin' but as soon as they stopped you had to stop. These ol' corncrakes'd go CARK! CARK! an' we'd move, then we'd stop ... just like musical chairs sort of thing, but we never did catch one did we?" He pauses, then continues. "Remember that other shepherd who used to live up at Park?"

"Baker," said Sid, "that was his name, I can tell you about Baker ... he was the broadest man ..."

"Oh, you've never heard anybody so ...," said Gordon, "mind, we were broad, but you could never understand one word out of ten with him."

"An' I'll tell you another thing before I forgets it," said Sid, "There was a get-me-round-the-strawberry, an' his name was Gaby Goddard zee, an' he used to take out the cake to the shepherd. Gaby wi' a 1914 pair o' Army breeches an' some puttees an' a Sergeant Majors's tunic wi' big pickets an' about three or four stripes. Well, the sheperd's dog jumped up at 'un an' he shouted, 'Get the bugger down!' - 'cause he was frightened, zee?"

"An' I'll tell you what he got us on ... this same shepherd zee," said Gordon, "Us boys, we'd often walk up to Park on a Sunday afternoon an' this shepherd would say, 'Now I can tell you bloody boys I can beat you at anything!' he said, 'I'll tell you what you can do. I'll give you an iron bar, now each of you can have ten hits in one hole zee? An' I'll bet I can go deeper in one than you can in ten ...' O' course if we'd a bleedin' thought we'd had known, but we didn't. So we all made holes, allus boys all along yere ... all along. Ten strikes each! Then he comes along wi' the bar an' struck in the same holes ... He just walked along behind us! One in this hole, one in that an' so on. An' they say that Wiltshire folk are daft!"

"But he were broad," said Sid, "real Wiltshire broad!"

Gladys joined in, "Do you remember that chap that pinched all the plums? An' the police were after him?"

"Floppy Wootton," said Sid.

"Yeh, Floppy Wootton," Gladys went on, "He was a tall gangly chap, an' he always had a fag. Well he had these Victoria plums, an' because they was after him, rather than throw them away, he ate them all! He had this great big bag an' as he went along he ate them all! An' he was in 'ospital next day!"

"Talkin' about Floppy Wootton," said Sid, "now that was the man I was talkin' to when war was declared. He used to work for the watercress people at Axford. An they were drillin' artesian wells just outside Southside Cottage. It was about three in the afternoon an' the drillers came over an' asked who I was talkin' to."

Sid was silent for a moment then he said, "I've just remembered some more nicknames. There was 'Sockey' an' 'Stoker' an' 'Uncle Nevvy' wi' a wooden leg an' then there was 'Shitty Dick', well that's what we used to call him!"

"Them were the days," said Gordon, "When Woodbines were tuppence for five ..."

"They was in a paper packet," said Sid.

"Fourpence for ten," Gordon when on, "an' there was some brands cheaper than that! Players were twenty for a shilling!"

"Can you remember the first time I started smokin'?" Sid asked, "We went down to feed the ol' pony on a Sunday afternoon. Of course you were a bit older than me Gordon, an' we got these Woodbines. Oh My God! An' I went home an' sat beside dad in the chair there an' gosh! Was I bad! It was terrible! Then, blow me! The week after, Gordon, you thought you'd smoke a pipe! An' then you wus as bad as what I was."

"We took one of Dad's pipes when he wasn't lookin'" said Gordon, "It only had a titchy little hole in the middle 'cause it was all furred up. We thought that it wouldn't 'old much 'baccer, p'raps a few dog-ends ... well I took it up to *The Castle* an' sat on the steps ... Blimey! Was I bad!"

"But we was always up to somethin'" said Sid, "we was always breakin' our necks. Once we had a three-wheeled trolley, - we had the original soap-box - 'twas made from Miss Osmond's old Bath Chair. We used to go up the woods an' load it up wi' firewood an' kindlin'. An' it was so steep comin' down, an' what wi' big stones an' that, well we never see'd this big stone an' we banged into the fence an' did a few somersaults!"

"An we went all the way over," Gordon laughed at the memory, "an' then, at the bottom, we unloaded all the wood an' went back up the top for another go!"

"'Twas those woods that had so many nuts weren't it?" Sid said, "Dad used to be the one for nuts an' mushrooms. You remember Gordon one night when he come in from *The Crown*, when he'd had a couple o' pints o' 4 x an' e' said that he was goin' to get up early the next mornin to go mushroomin', that was a Sunday mornin', an' you Gordon, fool-like said 'Saturday nights is different to Sunday mornings!' an' do you know, 'twas the only time I've seen my father really mad ... 'cause normally he was the most docile of men."

"But didn't he get a lot of mushrooms an' nuts," said Gordon, "Times we used to live on them! When we used to sleep two at the top an' two at the bottom, it war'nt the feet you had to worry about! 'Twas the nuts an' mushrooms!"

"Cause in them days," said Gladys, "We had nuts all the year round. Dad used to salt hem. We had a big brown crock he put hem in for christenings an' suchlike. Our Olive used to crack them in her hand, an' Ivy, next door, she'd always take a couple every day!"

"What wi' mushrooms an' nuts, plovers' eggs an' rabbits, not to mention trout an' the odd hare an' pheasant, we lived off the fat of the land!" Sid grinned at the thought.

"You had to in them days," said Gladys, "With Dad on the dole, there weren't much comin' in. I remember once when Mum had nothin left one Saturday, an' she sent young Olive up to the grocers for half a pint o' skimmed milk on tick, so as she could make a rice puddin' for Sunday dinner ... and do you know! They wouldn't let her have it! Poor Olive must have felt awful ... an' she was only a little kid!"

"Still, I expect the shopkeepers didn't have all that much themselves in them days," said Sid, "'cause its different now ain't it? But we never really went short!. Gordon, do you remember 'ow we used to put four bricks together down the garden? Like that!" He makes an imaginary square with his hands, "Wi' a tile on top, we had this special way o' setting it, to make a bird trap zee We had a thread so that when they tripped on't t'would drop. But if they didn't do it quick enough we had a long piece o' string."

"An we used to pluck them an' roast them in front of the fire," Gordon savoured the memory, "Beautiful they was, we used to do them on a stick. Like you say Sid, we lived off the fat of the land!"

"But us never did go much on snails, did we Gordon?" Sid grimaced at the thought, "but Jim told me t'other day, that his mum used to get them from under the stone walls near where they lived, put them in brine an' wash them 'orf, an' then boil them. An' if she had plenty she'd pickle some. An' she said they used to sit round the fire of a Saturday night, listenin' to the wireless an' hookin' their snails out wi' a pin! I wouldn't fancy that!" "Cause there was more meat about in them days," Gordon mused, "Not that it were cheap, although all the butchers used to slaughter their own."

"That's right," said Sid, "Me an' Fred Hall, we used to go, every Christmas, up to Alcot Farm, nearly to Newbury. Walk these two fat cattle back, an' the next day a feller used to come out from Hungerford, a one-eyed bloke wi' a patch, a great big feller, an' he used to put a rope roun' their horns, a loop roun' his muzzle an' pull his head down to a ring in the floor. An' then he'd hit him here." Sid pointed to the centre of his forehead, "Wi' a pole-axe ... Then he'd stir his brains up wi' a little cane!"

"Thats right," said Gordon, "That's just how they used to do it in them days."

A WALK BY THE RIVER

"Let's you an' me take a walk down to the river," said Sid, "Come on Gordon."

They both stood up. "Shan't be long Gladys," and they wandered off down Blind Lane, across the bottom of the road by The Knapp.

On reaching the river they leaned on the rails and looked at the fish flitting in the reed waving water below.

Gordon spoke first. "I was only thinkin' the other day Sid, of sixty an' seventy years ago when we used to come down to the river to take fish, an' old John Wootton, the water bailiff would come running after us. Mostly, of course we'd go down the river towards Newtown where they used to spawn." He paused to think. "But didn't we used to get some fish! I can remember mother cooking them even now."

Sid picked up a stone and threw it in the river.

"Well," he said, "We all had to do our best to help out in those hard times, an' in any case, if there was anything that looked like sport, we were there, weren't we? Why, when they went binderin' we'd all take sticks an' terriers an' get round the last bit, an' weren't there some rabbits in them days, I mean before they had myxy? I don't think that there wasn't a rabbit that was safe within three miles o' Blind Lane!"

"We had to make all our own tackle then," said Gordon, "What with snares an' catapults, remember how we'd cut out an ash or hazel prong, shape it up a bit, then drill two holes in it with a red hot knittin' needle, for the leather boot laces. An' we'd cut out a little knock in't so's you could slip it through an' knot it. An' then with a bit of an upper from an old shoe tied on with more leather laces. An' I used to shoot over the right stick ..." And he stretched out his left arm pulling the imaginary sling back to his cheek with his right hand.

Sid laughed. "An' sometimes," he said, "You shot an' 'it your thumb! Remember Gordon? We always held our thumb on top of the right stick, didn't we? Other folks would hold it low down but 'twas stronger at the top. An' for shot we used pebbles an' bits o'lead."

Gordon interrupted.

"I nearly always used bits o'iron cut off the rivetted ends o'tools, from down the foundry. They was terrible stuff really."

"Oh, I forgot that," said Sid, "An' warn't it heavy? If you every seed one o'us walkin' lop-sided, you'd know'd that we had a pocket full o'iron."

"I always used to aim for its eye," said Gordon.

"Ah the trick was," said Sid, "that we used to walk along an' say, see a rabbit at the side of the road, up a bank but we'd never stop, but go right on past an' then come back on the other side of the road. 'Cause that way we'd marked where he was, an' then, when you come back, he was ready. But if you'd stopped when you first saw 'un he was gone!"

"I can remember well one particular day," said Gordon, "You know White Hill where you go up by the Manor an' down towards Ma'lboro'? Well, when I worked for me dad wi' an ol' pony, well, I was drivin' down this hill wi' a load of stuff one mornin', an' I saw this rabbit on the other side of the road a settin' on the bank, an' I knew he was mine! So s'now, when we were comin' back up the 'ill I let th' ol' pony walk on in front an' I walked behind ... an' blowed if I didn't knock him straight out o' there! Right down the bank! A beautiful bit o' work!"

Sid turned to face the sun and leant back on the bridge rails.

"But I s'pose," he said, "we must have caught most rabbits in wire. Do you remember how we used to make rabbit wires from a beam in the pantry?"

Gordon smiles at the memory and nodded. "Ah," he said, "used to make th'old wires from a hook in the beam."

"Wi' a flat iron!" Sid said.

"Ah, a flat iron to keep the wires 'angin' straight. Three turns round, that made six wires, then two spins, an' that were a rabbit snare made!"

Sid turned again to look down the river.

"You know Gordon," he said, "the best night I ever had wi' snares was when I was keeperin'. One night I got eleven rabbits wi' thirteen snares. I'd set these thirteen wires zee, in runs across the corner of the field where they come out of the wood. An' I went round at six o'clock an' took so many out, an' I went roun' again at twelve o'clock. 'Cause it was only about three hundred yards from where we lived, an' then I went round in the mornin'. Eleven rabbits from thirteen wires! Just think!"

He looked round at Gordon. "I mean," he went on, "I reckoned if you could average three rabbits from ten wires you were doin' well... But I used to go roun' my wires regular s'now. Most folk only go roun' once a day."

"Puttin' wires down were alright," said Gordon, "but there's nothin' like a bit o' ferretin' about February time."

"Do you remember how, on a dark night, after the pheasants had gone up, you could go round with a torch an' knock them off with a stick?"

Gordon nodded his head, looked towards Spring Hill and went on, "Mind some nights we used to go up there to old Wilson's stacks, remember how the hares used to run?"

"Only too well," said Sid, "One time we went up there was the first week I went to work an' had two bob in me pocket."

"'Twas quite a lot in them days ..."

"Anyways, you an' me Gordon we were goin' up Spring 'ill as usual on a Saturday afternoon, a rabbitin' ... o' course," he corrects his memory, "it warn't night at all ... well, it seems that I got took short!, an' when I had me trousers down I went an' lost me two bob. When I found I'd lost it we was back home! But we went back up th'ill an' searched for it! Mind, we'd follow our noses, but we never did find it. I expect its still there!"

"Then remember how we used to go plover nestin'," said Gordon, pointing down the valley, "six of us used to go together ..."

"Ah, we used to do it properly," said Sid, "six of us strung out across this field ..."

"We made a proper job of it," emphasised Gordon.

"When out comes this keeper ...!"

"You're forgetting' Sid," said Gordon, "We run! An' when we got down by the wood, there they was! Keepers on both sides! An' as we went by they belted the big ones ..."

"But me an' another small boy got orf," Sid grinned, "Just because we was small. But 'twas we who was carrying' the eggs!" He paused for thought then went on, "But the police never worried us did they? 'Twas keepers really ... 'twas the same when I was a keeperin' meself, before the war when I lived at Axford. Do you remember ol' Batten, the copper? He was my mate; we used to go down to *The Crown*, an' as soon as he had a couple o' pints he used to talk as if he had a dozen marbles in his mouth. I used to leave my bicycle at his place in Blow'orn Street; 'cause I went there to see if he'd go beatin' wi' us! Well, that was my excuse to go in! Ol' Batten was alright, but his wife was just the reverse, an' she used to create Merry Hell when I went up there wi' him. But there's one thing I remember about ol' Batten, there was a 'wanted', I don't remember whether he was a murderer or not, but he was a well-wanted man, an' ol' Batten caught him over by The Golden Arrow Cafe. O' course Batten never got the praise for it, somebody else got the praise, somebody a little bit higher up. Old Batten was only an ordinary copper! Talkin' about policemen, do you remember that copper who said that he used to put down rabbit wires when he was on the beat? Then he'd go an' turn the pubs out at closin' time an' go round his wires before he went home. One night, when he was goin' round the wires with another copper, the Sergeant's motor turned up. T'other feller got up an' started to run but the first un grabbed his tunic an' pulled him down. 'Where'st be gwoine?' he said, 'I don't want to be caught poachin',' said 'other. 'You ain't poachin'!' said the first one, 'You ain't a poacher! You're a policeman! ... You're lookin' for a poacher!'"

Gordon smiled and slapped the handrail of the bridge. "You know Sid," he said, "Whenever I think of this bridge I always remember that poem we all had to learn at school. Can you remember it?"

Sid nodded, and they both continued ...

"Then out spake brave Horatius,
The Captain of the Gate;
'To every man upon this earth
Death cometh soon or late.
And how can man die better
Than facing fearful odds,
For the ashes of his fathers, And the temples of his Gods?'

They both paused, flushed with the spirit of the poem and then went on ...

'Hew down the bridge, Sir Consul,
With all the speed ye may;
I, with two more to help me, will hold the foe in play.
In yon strait path a thousand
May well be stopped by three.
Now who will stand on either hand,
And keep the bridge with me?'"

Smiling with the satisfaction of having remembered so well and so long they slapped the handrail again and turned to face the setting sun. The wind blew chill down the river.

"'Tis cold," said Sid, "I'm proper shrammed, let's be gwoine."

And they both walked slowly towards the village square.

DIALOGUES

OLIVE AND GLADYS

Although some memories of the old home of childhood seem crystal-clear it often becomes difficult, when put to the test, to recall them in exact detail. One night after supper, with a jug of home-made wine, Gladys and Olive resolved to describe number two Mount Pleasant, Ramsbury in detail. It was forty years since either of them had lived there. This is the conversation which followed.

Gladys

"Just as you go in the front door there was an ordinary wooden chair. But, if anybody was comin' a leather chair came down from the bedroom, didn't it?

Then there was a wooden cupboard, that Uncle Mark 'ad made for his tea. That's Uncle Mark an' Aunt Harriet that brought Mum up ... When she made us scrub it out we were told that Uncle Mark had it for his tea. [Pauses] On the cupboard was a glass dish ..."

Olive

"And two black china elephants ..."

Gladys and Olive together,

"A horseshoe shaped mirror ..."

Gladys

"With flowers painted down the side, Gordon's pot of Vicilma cream, Gordon used to have, it was a green pot, an' I used to pinch it! ... [Thinks] What else was there?"

Olive

"The baker's book on the right hand side at the back ..."

Gladys

"'Cause he used to come in an' put down what you had every day. [Pauses] An' ... Dad's tobacco jar ... a coloured Paisley tobacco jar. That was in the middle ... On the wall ... pictures of Aunt Harriet and Uncle Mark ..."

Olive

"Weren't they at the top? ... They were! I know that they were eventually put in the pantry!"

Gladys carries on.

"In the middle of the back wall was the pantry door. An' on the right a chest of drawers where we kep' all the sheets an' blankets an' linen ... with all the papers an' photographs.

On the chest of drawers? I'm blowed if I can remember! Oh! I know! There was a photograph of Mum an' Dad when they married. Mum with a straight straw hat an' a blouse with leg o' mutton sleeves. A tight leather belt, an' a full skirt. Dad 'ad a little round bowler, not a proper one, a tiny round bowler hat an' a black coat an' striped trousers. It was in black an' white, but it was quite good! Not in a silver frame, but the kind of frame ... well, you slipped the photo behind the glass. You know the short of thing!"

Olive

"Over Uncle Mark's cupboard was a clock!"

Gladys

"Like a school clock!"

Olive

"With a little pendulum ..."

Gladys

"With Roman numerals."

Olive

"Dad used to lay the clock down on its back when it wouldn't go an' oil the works with the tip of a feather dipped in paraffin."

[Both are silent trying to remember]

Gladys

"I can't remember what was on the left hand side of the pantry door ..."

Olive

"No I can't either ... but there was a chair just in ..."

Gladys interrupts

"Yes, just in front there was a chair that came down. A low sort of armchair. A best chair it was with wooden arms. There was a Windsor chair there first when we was kids. I don't know why they changed it! ... You know, a tall, old-fashioned Windsor chair.

On the left hand side of the room was a fireplace. An open fire with a tiny oven on the right hand side, and on the left a mock thing to even it up. Dad made a piece of iron to sit across the top for kettles an' saucepans."

Olive

"An' the flames an' smoke just leapt the space an' up the chimney!"

Gladys

"In front was a steel fender an' steel fire-irons. Very highly polished! 'Twas the bane of our lives wasn't it Olive? We cleaned them with emery first, every little mark, an' then with Silvo. I don't know where they come from, perhaps Dad made them. But woe betide you if the kettle spat out a bit of rust! We had to get in an' wipe it off straight away!"

Olive

"Above the fireplace, round the mantle shelf was a plush pelmet with bobbles on, nailed on with brass headed nails."

Gladys

"An' on the shelf there were two tall black tins. I'm sure that they must have been something to do with the tea!"

Olive

"An' two black horses ... or were they on the cupboard at the side?"

Gladys

"They were the ones Dad got from Osmonds when they packed up Foundry House ..."

Olive

"There used to be a small clock ..."

Gladys

"Just an ordinary little clock, wasn't it? 'cause we went by the big clock ... An' there was some sort of ornaments, animals I think ..."

Olive

"On the right side of the fireplace was a cupboard."

Gladys

"In the bottom we kept God knows what! Anything we wanted to hide away! An' at the top there was a place with hooks where we kept the china."

Olive

"An' right by the fire was the wood cupboard ..."

Gladys [laughs]

"That was full of beetles! The beetles used to come out at night an' Dad used to put down red lead, didn't he?"

Olive

"There was two cupboards on the left hand side!"

Gladys

"That's right!"

Olive

"One up an' one down."

Gladys

"We used to keep books there, an' things we all had. Dad's books, an' Gordon's books an' Sid's books. You know, like *Robinson Crusoe*!".

Olive

"Under the window at the front there used to be a couch."

Gladys

"'Til mother's bed went there ..."

Olive

"And on the window ledge were plants."

Gladys

"Loads of plants! Sid kept a lot from Ramsbury Manor, didn't he? 'Cause when her bed was there, she used to have a little garden in the window, didn't she?"

Olive

"And at the foot of the bed, just inside the front door, was a screen with a canary cage on it. The canary's name was Joey!"

Gladys [laughing]

"Joey! ... Dad's pride an' joy!"

Olive

"The screen used to be papered and in the winter there was a dark green plush or baize curtain that was drawn across from the screen to shut off the front door."

Gladys

"An' we mustn't forget the curtains on the window. In the summer, ... just lace ones. The window wasn't very big but there always seemed to be enough light, but in the winter, a paraffin lamp with a tall chimney stood on the middle of the table."

Olive

"That's right! We've forgotten the table. That was a square deal table. The sort with scrubbed top an' varnished legs!"

Gladys

"An' there were always a few rail back chairs but Dad had a special one with short legs that he used to sit on close to the fire, smokin' his pipe."

Olive [reflecting]

"That's about it in the front room! But through the pantry door there was, ... at the back, on the right hand wall ... those pictures of Uncle Mark an' Aunt Harriet whose eyes seemed to follow you everywhere! Behind the door, on the right, was a meat-safe hung on the wall. And, next to that, a table covered with rexine."

Gladys

"There was a shelf at the top with saucepans on ..."

Olive

"At the back under the window? Was there a bowl?"

Gladys

"Yes, under the window on a little table with a drop-leaf."

Olive

"An' a bucket for the slops!"

Gladys

"A bucket of fresh water stood in the corner, an' there was a big earthenware pan. We used to get water from the well an' fill up the pan, didn't we."

Olive

"That's right."

Gladys

"At the side stood an enamel jug, an' you used it to fill up the kettle from the pan of water."

Olive

"On the left side of the pantry under the stairs was where mother used to hide when we had thunder an' lightening ... She used to take me in there ..."

Gladys [laughing]

"She used to take us all in there!"

Olive [incredulously]

"In the little hole under the stairs with all the cardboard boxes!"

Gladys

"She was scared. [Pauses] She was! An' you see the trouble that follows! I've often spoken about that to my children. Because she was frightened, I'm a little bit frightened too! Simply because she took us in there! ... Just as soon as it thundered, you ran upstairs an' threw something - a cloth - over the mirrors. Put all the knives an' forks out of sight, an' the scissors! [Laughs and continues incredulously] The scissors, 'anging by the mantlepiece, and we had to cover [and suddenly remembers] an' Oh! the brush an' comb bag!"

Olive

"Yes, that's right."

Gladys

"By the side of the mantlepiece, an' the scissors hung on the same hook."

Olive

"I've just remembered what was on the left hand side of the pantry door in the front room ... it was Mum's treadle sewing machine!"

Gladys

"That's right Olive! A Singer!"

[Pauses and continues with the contents of the pantry]

"Then there was the stairs. They was just inside the pantry on the left. Straight up an' down. Eight stairs!"

Olive [confirms]

"Eight stairs!"

Gladys

"Scrubbed at first, until we had carpet. An' when you got to the top, a tiny square landin', like that [she holds her hands three feet apart] wasn't it? No bigger than that Olive!

On the right at the top was the back bedroom."

Gladys

"It only had a partition about three or four feet high, for a bit of privacy. You could almost see the bed from the landin' but you could see the dressin' table ..."

Olive

"In the window ...

Gladys [nods confirmation]

In the window at the top of the bed. The back bedroom was a sort of extension of the landin', very small, but there was always a double bed in there ... 'Cause there was enough of us to sleep ... Two at the top an' two at the bottom! Wasn't it? An' a little single bed that way [makes an angle motion with her hands] Olive would have a single bed! ... When we were small, in the double bed there was Gordon an' Sid at the top an' Doris an' I at the bottom. Hilda must have gone by then I suppose ..."

Olive [resuming the description of the house]

"At the top of the stairs, on the left, was Mum's room. With a door! There was two double beds in that room!"

Gladys

"At one time there was Mum an' Dad in there an' Doris an' I."

Olive

"And me!"

Gladys [nods]

"And you! ... After your mum an' George ..."

Olive

"At one time I slept between you an' Doris!"

Gladys [not hearing Olive's comment continues]

"George an' Hilda, yer mum, slept in the back room. 'Cause you were born there ... in the back room in the double bed."

Olive, [persisting]

"I can remember sleeping between you an' Doris in the front bedroom, an' it must have been Sid sleepin' in the back bedroom."

Gladys, [thinks]

"Um! Yes. As he grew up. That must have been after your mum went away an' Gordon had gone to Kent."

Olive [sticking to her subject]

"What I never liked about that was, being younger, I always had to come to bed first. Into a cold bed! An' on a cold winter's night when there was only one fire in the house it was ... Oh! [she shudders] ... real terrible!"

Gladys

"There was a chair in between, an' a box along the window."

Olive

"An' a washstand."

Gladys

"An' a dressing table an' everything, so they weren't bad times really ..."

Olive [still thinking about the cold bed]

"What used to annoy me was I was always sent up first to warm the bed before you two came up."

Gladys

"Wasn't fair was it?"

Olive

"When I remember going home last, unexpectedly, Doris and Jim were in the back room. Mum and Dad were in the front room, and the only place I could sleep was on that rexine settee. I don't know how it got upstairs ... between the chimney and the wall ... where the window was ... along there ... and I slept on it!"

Gladys

"The blanket box in Mum's room had a little tin in the side we called the 'till'. An' we kep' all the papers in it. Well, you know, the marriage certificates an' the birth certificates, an' the death certificates. It was an ordinary wooden box with this little piece in the side, wasn't it?"

Olive

"Yes! An' by the chimney breast there was a tin trunk."

Gladys

"The old tin trunk where we used to keep blankets and clothes an' stuff. Best suits! Best clothes!"

Olive

"And Best hats!"

Gladys

"That's right!, anniversary hats! Some in boxes, very long cardboard boxes. An' that reminds me! Gordon used to buy his girlfriend, Dorothy Goodman who worked at Knighton Farm, a quarter pound o' chocolates an' some roses to take to her every Sunday, an' I used to nip in there an' pinch a couple! As soon as I saw him put 'em in there I was up there behind him. He knew I did it!

There was always a couple missin'!"

Having exhausted their memories of the house, Gladys and Olive turn their thoughts to the garden.

Olive

"There was no garden at the back of the house only somebody's field. The garden was at the front. Under the front window there was just a small strip."

Gladys

"With lots of periwinkles and stocks."

Olive

"And the garden path going straight down from the front door with wooden railings."

Gladys

"Then the sawing horse."

Olive

"Yes, but before that, was the flower garden where Sid used to grow his special flowers. Then, the kitchen garden with cabbages and runner beans and things, then there was the ash-pit. That used to have the bucket emptied into it every week an' the ashes from the fire put on top."

Gladys

"We used to keep a few chickens at the bottom of the garden just at the back of the loos. When your mum was at Aldbourne Dad often used to kill a chicken. I can remember him killing a chicken. He used to pluck it, an' Mum would draw an' dress it, an' I'd take the chicken, an' a few potatoes perhaps, or whatever Mum could spare an' walk to Aldbourne with it. You know, over to The Butts, where Auntie Lou was. An' sometimes I'd walk over The Southard, as they call it, up Loves Lane an' then come out by The Butts. Of course, you were only a baby then Olive. I can remember once when you were there an' you were on yer mum's knee an' you pulled the table-cloth an' the teapot went right over! Your mum went mad! I held you while your mum cleared it all up. In the evening I'd walk back to Ramsbury. Sometimes I'd stay the night. They had a bed-chair like the one we had at home. Hilda used to bring me down a pillow an' a blanket an' I'd stay ... then walk back in the morning. I wasn't very old but I didn't think anything of it! When your father was so ill, Mum used to worry about you having enough to eat. I mean, George was in an' out of work an' eventually he went off to a Sanatorium at Farnham in Surrey where he died. [Pauses]

An' you were so ill as a baby Olive ..."

Olive

"I had pluerisy ..."

Gladys [incredulous]

"You didn't have pluerisy, did you Olive?"

Olive, [emphatic]

"I had pneumonia AND pleurisy. I can never remember which I had first ... THEN mastoid! ALL before I was three!"

Gladys

"I can remember when you went to hospital. You had a little pink sponge-cloth skirt an' a pink jumper. I remember standing you on the table."

Olive

"I can remember being taken to hospital."

Gladys

"Yes, Savernake ..."

Olive

"An' you leavin' me on the bed in the Matron's room. She was sitting at the table taking down the particulars ... an' me just screaming me head off!"

Gladys

"That's right."

Olive

"'Cause you were all going, leaving me!"

Gladys

"They wouldn't let us come an' see you! Gordon an' them used to come over, did't they?"

Olive

"Gordon came to see me. I can remember him coming with someone else. I don't know who was with him, but both of them had a shock of dark, wavy hair. I can remember him standin' a the bottom of my cot."

Gladys

"Wasn't it Bert Giddings?"

Olive

"I don't think it was ..."

Gladys

"I think it was Bert Giddings ..."

Olive

"An' I can remember bein' there at Christmas time, an' all of the ones that were capable of standin' up, standing on a mattress in the corner. Father Christmas came in with a bag on his back. I was given a doll rather like a golliwog with a painted face that I proceeded to wet. [Laughs] It looked all-over alike when I'd finished with it! An' I can remember being taken to the bathroom by Nurse Nightingale. She used to have to take me through the men's ward an' when I came back there was a chap on the right hand side of the door, an' always, on the top of his locker, was about six or seven dolly mixtures. Funny thing about the name Nightingale, our son Tony went to Savernake with bad scalds about twenty-five years after I was there, he was only about three, but because he had to have skin grafts they sent him to Stoke Mandeville. There he was looked after by a Nurse Nightingale!"

Gladys

"When you were in Savernake I used to ride in from Ramsbury on a bike ..."

Olive

"I can't remember you coming in!"

Gladys

"They wouldn't let us in the ward! We could look through a little window! You cried so much the first time!"

Olive

"I can remember someone an' my mother an' Aunt Emily, all in the back of this doctor's car, taking me to Savernake Hospital."

Gladys

"It was a big, funny old car."

Olive

"You could get three in the back!"

Gladys

"It had one of those hoods, a big, canvassy one. I don't know what the car was called, I was only interested in riding in it. It was the only way we could get there then. There was no ambulance! But when I came in to see you I used to go to Costers an' say 'Can I have a bike to go an' see Olive?' Fancy cycling all up Manor Hill?"

Olive

"When I first started work in Ma'lborough I used to cycle home on half days an' cycle back again at night! In the middle of winter as well! The place where I worked was Preshute along by Manton. An' there was another place on the right at the end, by the church. In the first one there was about twenty-five boys, an' in the second about fifty! I was only about sixteen!"

Gladys

"Did you see that thing on the box the other night? About colleges? The boys were talkin' about the girls that worked there. They thought that the girls that worked in the college were more attractive than those that they found in the town. How did you cope Olive?"

Olive

"The boys were only interested in each other in those days! They used to disappear into the wood up the top! Of course I was innocent! I didn't know what they were doing! But I know now!"

Gladys [laughing]

"When I was young I thought I knew it all! But I knew nothing! We weren't told like the kids are today. They do know where they're goin' but I was the same as you Olive, when 'that' started I went downstairs an' Mum said, 'Here you are, you use that.' An' that was it! God! Why ever didn't we get into trouble? Your parents didn't tell you anything! An' nowadays, they know it all! I think that the boys in Ramsbury were frightened of getting us into trouble. They thought of the seven and six a week they'd have to pay!

We were just told, 'If you get into trouble, don't darken my doors!' But then, we didn't know what trouble was really."

Olive

"When I was small the boys I used to play with were Leslie Westall, Bob Brown, an' Tony Giddings. Doris used to ask me what we did when we played together! I think she only tried to find out to tell Mum!"

Gladys

"Do you remember Mabel Westall who lived down the road from us? Mabel Westall, Mary Watts and me were the same age. Mary Watts, that was at Whittonditch, was governess or something to those folk round the back by Admiral Hyde Parker's at Parliament Piece. What was their names?"

Olive

"Was it Wyndham? One of them's just written a book. I think it's called 'Love Lessons'."

Gladys

"I can remember a boy at *The Windsor Castle* who caught ringworm. He used to wear a woolly hat, an' I had to go an' play with him! I think that that was when Dad used to go to that pub. I expect he said 'I'll send our Gladys to play with him!' But when I was older, if ever I wanted to go out, such as if there was a dance at the Memorial Hall, that'd be when I was working for Doctor Kellet, to get Dad in a good mood I'd give him the money for an ounce of tobacco. Talk about! Just so I could stay out 'till ten!"

GORDON AT TONBRIDGE

During a visit to Gordon's home at Tonbridge where he has lived for many years, Olive asked him to read all of the foregoing record, and then to add some contribution by way of comment and further reminiscence.

Gordon, now eighty years old, had much to remember and conversed subsequently, at various times, for over ten hours. Being nearly sixteen years older than Olive his memories of life in Ramsbury and at the family home are different by a generation. His opening remarks concern a harmonium which lends a new dimension (of music) to life at number two Mount Pleasant. Memories of the jobs he had after leaving school, as house-boy-cum-rabbit-catcher for the Wilsons, or as a ploughboy with Bert Giddings at Knighton Farm, contrast strongly with his life when he moved to Kent in 1927. His account of life in Kent follows on after his memories of Ramsbury.

Olive after leaving
Savernake Hospital.

Ramsbury Church c1920.

Upper Mill c1910.

MUSICAL EVENINGS

Gordon

"Now, you probably don't remember this Olive, but you mentioned in your conversation with Gladys what was on the left-hand side of the pantry door at home. Well I can remember when there was a harmonium there, which mother would play on a Sunday night, and we used to sing Sankey an' Moody hymns. There was 'Shall we gather at the River?' and 'When the roll is called up yonder I'll be there!' And they had one that I don't believe was a proper hymn, it was", he pauses to think, and then continues, - singing ...

"The train will stop an' take you in at any station on the line,

Will you go? Will you go?

Oh! Go to that beautiful land with me!

[His voice rises at the end of this line]

Will you go? Will you go?

Oh! Go to that beautiful land!

I remember my dad singing that as well as anything. Dad would sit, smoking his pipe, on his short-legged chair in front of the fire. Sometimes, when mother was playing she would turn round to him an' say 'Harry, you're not singing!' an' he'd slowly take his pipe from his mouth and sing 'Pom! Pom! Pom!', real tuneful like. That was his contribution!

We had tea at four o'clock, always! Sharp at four o'clock! Dinner at twelve, tea at four, and, although the lamp probably wouldn't be lit, we'd have the fire alight, an' we'd sit there for an hour an' sing all these Sankey an' Moody hymns. And nowadays, you can't imagine children sitting down an' doing that! Well, there was no other enjoyment then, was there? An' then, at about seven o'clock, if he had a bob or two in his pocket, Dad'd wander up towards *The Crown*. But that harmonium, Olive, I can remember that clearly, but there's probably things that you remember that I don't. As I say, comin' away when I was twenty-one in 1927 an' you livin' there afterwards, you'll remember a lot more things than what I do. I mean, there's things mentioned in there [pointing to the unfinished typescript] that I didn't know anything about! No I don't remember them, but Gladys, she's got it all down pretty good! All about Charlie Sparrow the Ramsbury Poet, an' these games we used to have round at his house. I mean, he'd be called 'gay' nowadays, but he really wasn't, you know! 'E loved boys! [He laughs] But that's what they'd call him now, they'd call him 'gay'!"

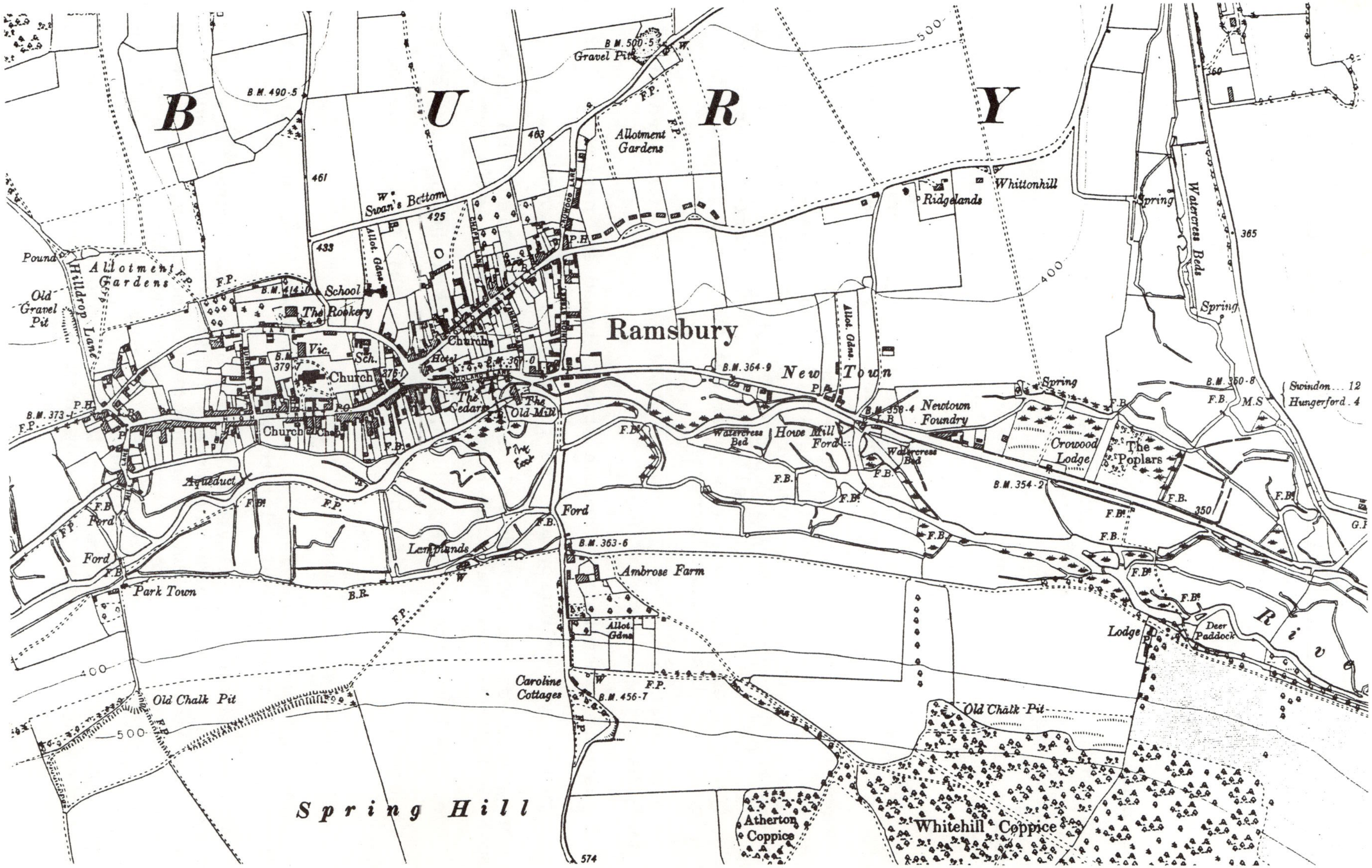

Ramsbury in 1925 from the 3rd edition of the Ordnance Survey 1:10,000 map

POACHING FOR A LIVING

Gordon

"There's one chap I'll always remember, that's the one we called Shimball. I'll always remember him because he took me rabbit catchin', as Sid said, the first time ever I'd gone. An' that was up Loves Lane an' into a pit! This was one Saturday afternoon in the middle of winter. He put this ferret in a hole in the pit an' of course nothin' came out! We sat there about half hour an' then he said, 'I'll go an' have a look round. You sit there boy!'

Well, I sat there an' waited an' this bloomin' dog come up, an' a chap with a gun under his arm. I was frightened out of me life! I kep' quiet, an' he didn't see me but as soon as he went, I went!

When I got home, Shimball came in an' said, 'What about the ferret?' An' I said that it'd never came out! Shimball went up on the Sunday mornin' but he never found it. Thinkin' about it since, it was the daftest place you could ever put a ferret in! One single hole in the side of a pit! Well I mean, if the ferret ever got over the top of those rabbits, it'd never get out until it had eaten its way out! But that's what happened.

Old Shimball used to sing quite a bit, there was his version of 'Molly Malone', it went ...

I pushed my wheelbarrow through streets broad an' narrow

I pushed my wheelbarrow an' the front wheel went round!

An' there was another one he'd sing. It was called 'The Prickalie Bush'. I don't know what that meant, but it went - let's see ...

Over the bush, the prickalie bush, it pricks my heart quite sore,

If every I get out of the prickalie bush, I'll never get in anymore.

That's all I can remember.

Shimball used to come in to us a lot. Mother used to write letters for him. Not that he had a lot to write!

When we were boys we played a lot out of school hours but we seldom played with anybody below the tree. [This refers to an ancient elm tree that stood in The Square in the centre of the village.] We was always 'our end' but there weren't many of the boys below the tree who went poachin' like Sid an' me. We spent all our wakin' hours poachin'. Well I suppose you wouldn't call it poachin', [he considers for a minute], but in a way I suppose it was. I remember I was once with him an' Bob Lockey up at Eastridge after peewits' eggs.

On the way home there was a place where we had to come down a ride with palings on either side, when we saw a keeper standin' at the bottom! We turned round quick to run back, an' blow me if there wasn't another keeper standin' at the top!

We were trapped!

We know straight away that we were for it!

There was nowhere to run! We were too small to get over those palings!

Well, these keepers started to thump us an' poor old Bob had some boils on the back of his neck, an' I can always remember his shoutin' out 'Mind me boils! Mind me boils!'

I didn't escape scot free either! The other keeper had a lump of wood and he caught me a hell of a wallop on the backside!

Served us right, I suppose!"

Olive

"Perhaps it was for the excitement, but it was need as well, after all you know that it you caught a rabbit, you'd have rabbit for dinner! You must have walked miles after rabbits!"

Gordon

"We always walked, we walked everywhere. There was no cars. Places like Stock Close you'd never see a soul. Mind, we had to keep out of the gamekeepers' way but we always got a rabbit an' sometimes a pheasant. If there was a pheasant in the hedge, we'd get it! That's if we could shoot straight enough! There was rabbits an' pheasants in the winter an' moorhens' eggs in the spring.

We used to get dozens of moorhens' eggs! We had a system where we used to tie a table spoon on the end of a long stick. When the nest was too far out in the water we used to push the spoon out an' tip an egg into it, one egg at a time. Then we had another system. McDougals' flour in them days used to come in small linen bags, well, we'd get an empty flour bag an' bend a piece of wire round the top an' make it like a butterfly net, then put that on the end of a long stick an' push that out to the nest. We could get a half dozen eggs into it at one time!

On a Saturday afternoon Dad used to get down the 'ole fryin' pan an' fill it up! Smashin'!"

Olive

"I was just thinkin' about what you were sayin' about not playin' with the boys who lived below the tree. When I was there as a child, fifteen years after you were there Gordon, we didn't play with the children who lived in the High Street. Those who lived below *The Bell* were strangers! An' when the Council houses were built, even the children there were strangers. We just played with a few close by. Well, in The Lane I suppose."

Gordon

"That's right Olive, but the strange thing was that we always played with the others at school, but not out of school hours. We just used to be this one clique. Bob Lockey, Siddy Westall, Johnny Westall, all up this top end. But we weren't all bad. After poachin' on Sunday morning' we used to have to go to Sunday School. I was in the choir for quite a time. Later on Sid an' I used to go snarin' at Short Pieces an' that's when we started to make these rabbit wires. Gladys said that the hook we used was still over the lintel when she went back to Mount Pleasant recently.

I remember one Saturday afternoon we walked down to Whittonditch an' I said to Sid, 'Look at those runs out there!' So we went home an' I believe I borrowed sixpence off Mother, an' I went down to old Pettifer Carter's shop, an' we bought a hank of brass wire. Well, then we went home an' made these wires. I don't know how old we was, we couldn't have been very old, I know we was still at school. Well, we went an' set these snares on the Saturday an' on the Sunday mornin' we got up almost as soon as it was light, an' I forget how many rabbits we had but it was a good load. Then, when we was comin' back home, the keeper from Crowood came down the path from Little Wood. We didn't know what to do. I said to Sid, 'Lie down!', an' we laid down in this grass an' watched him go right down the road an' he never saw us!

An' that was the first start of this poachin'!

After that, we used to do everything really, fishin', gettin' plovers' eggs, snarin', shootin' with catapults an' throwin' with a stone. We used to be pretty good with a stone. I mean a rabbit was really somethin', there was always a good meal in a rabbit!"

Olive

"If we hadn't had rabbits we wouldn't have had much meat in those days!"

Gordon

"We only had butcher's meat once a week. Mother couldn't afford any more. I don't suppose anybody could, but some people kept a pig. I remember old Granny Giddings boiling up potatoes for their pig. Those pigs were kept no more than twenty yards from her front door in this sty, an' the manure was chucked out in a heap. Can you imagine anybody puttin' up with that nowadays? [Pauses] I can still see that pig bein' got out. They was fat! They really were fat!"

Olive

"I remember I was goin' to school with Doris one afternoon, an' I was runnin' down the court at the side of the house, when I kicked a stone or something and I fell over an' I cut my knee open! I went screamin' my head off back up to Mum and she said 'Now you won't be able to go to school,' an' she stuck a bandage round me knee. But I didn't mind because I was allowed to stand up in a chair and look out of the window, because that it was that afternoon they were killin' Granny Giddings' pig."

Gordon

"It was quite a business, killin' a pig. Old Pigsticker Winchcombe used to come up didn't he? They used to get the ol' pigs up on this long stool, purposely made, an' stick the knife in, an' then it was put on a haulm of straw an' all set alight. I can remember pullin' its toenails off. They used to be 'prugged', hung up, an' they used to split it down the middle.

The next day he'd come up an they'd cut it up in joints an' everybody who had contributed when it was alive had a bit of it when it was dead. I reckon pig's liver doesn't taste the same now as it did when we were kids. Perhaps that was it, I mean when you're a kid an' you're hungry all the time everything tastes so much better. I remember those faggots that Granny Giddings used to make, she used to make some beautiful faggots, they always had a little bit of fat on the top. Then there was the bladder an' the lard. We used to try an' get this bladder an' make a football with it."

Olive

"These modern massed produced foods just don't taste the same. When Dad went beatin' up at Park he used to come home with a bit of venison sometimes, we lived high then."

Gordon

"Even during the first war we were never really hungry. There was always a rabbit, there was always moorhens' eggs, whatever it was, as far as we was concerned there was no 'in season' or 'out of season'. There was always something you could get. I used to kill trout when they was spawnin' up the river in about two inches of water. Kill them with a stone from a catapult an' take them home, an' mother used to fry them in the ol' fryin' pan. They used to be lovely. That reminds me Olive, you remember Dad made a trivet for the front of the fire. You could put a plate on it. Mother used to buy him bloaters sometimes an' he used to toast these bloaters with all the fat drippin' out on the plate underneath. It was lovely! Oh! beautiful!"

Olive

"Toast made these days never tastes the same does it?"

Gordon

"Toast now is only 'browned' bread, but toast then was totally different. When he used to have an egg he used to dip us in a bit of bread with yolk on it."

Olive

"In the summer when he'd been out working all day he used to come home an' have cold potatoes, broad beans and meat, an' I always used to have some of his, I used to love it!"

Gordon

"Broad beans were his favourite. He would often take broad beans, cold to work, in one of Rosier's blue sugar bags, an' eat them like sweets, one at a time."

Olive

"Sweets were a treat and Mum didn't buy any tinned vegetables, we always grew a year's supply in the garden or on the allotment."

Gordon

"The first tinned stuff that I can remember was in the 1914-18 War when the cavalry were on the racecourse. We used to go out there an' 'twas then that they gave us a tin of jam. They called it 'pozzy'! An' that's the first tinned food that I ever saw.

That was the cavalry. They used to bring their horses down to old Bill Watts at the bottom of The Lane to have them shod. An' I can remember one of their horses gettin' killed outside *The Bell*. They used to take them down to the front of the Mill House where they could ride them into the water. But this time they were comin' by *The Bell* an' one chap was ridin' one an' leadin' about six others, an' one of them jumped over just as a pony trap was comin' by an' the shaft of the pony trap ran into it, an' they killed him! Outside *The Bell*! It was the first time I'd seen a dead horse!"

MY FIRST JOBS

Olive

"What did you do when you left school?"

Gordon

"Well, it was a sort of combination of two jobs. I went to work as a sort of house-boy at Axford Farm for Bert Wilson's sister. I remember he had three sisters. I used to brush the stairs down an' polish the brass, those sort of things. That was in the summer. Then, in the winter, I used to catch the rabbits on all his brother's farms. See, I started goin' with Jim Bull catchin' these rabbits. He made me carry the ferrets.

Jim Bull married Florrie Woolford who was the daughter of the man at *The Boot*. Jim Bull had been a time-serving soldier an' came out of the Army just after the First World War. He was a proper Sergeant-Major, the way he walked an' they way he started off, his bearing an' everything. He was a proper Sergeant-Major!"

Olive

"That's why he made you carry the ferrets! How many did you use? Two or three?

Gordon

"Four! In case we lost one! I carried them in bags with a bit of straw at the bottom, an' then you had probably six or seven dozen nets, purse nets. The spade an' the iron bar we didn't carry home every day, we used to hide them, although it wouldn't have mattered, there was never anyone about."

Olive

"Did you ferret the same places all the time?"

Gordon

"Oh no, you'd move on. You did it in rotation. Sometimes it was to opposite side of Ramsbury all around Kessy Bottom (that's Kearsdown Farm over Axford) or New Buildings, or Pentico, all up round there. We were doing it on a sort of contract. Jim Bull was workin' for Bert Wilson whose brother George owned all the farms, all the way round. Wilsons had a field called Hundred Acres at Aldbourne, it was ploughed-up in 1918, during the War and they cut the corn, wheat, on an August Bank Holiday. All in one day! They'd got fourteen self-binders! But then some farmers, especially when several relations farmed in the same area would often pool their tackle to do a big job. It was on such a Field Day at the Gores that Bert Giddings once counted fifty-four horses working in the same field!

Olive

"But a hundred acres of sheaves took some shockin'-up!"

Gordon

"Well they didn't trouble about that, not for a day or two, but these was all these binders an' all these horses from all his farms all the way round."

Olive

"One of the Wilsons died in 1985. Did you know? I think he lived at Rudge Farm, up over Spring Hill."

Gordon

"He'd be the grandson of the ones I'm talkin' about. George Wilson was the father, Ted Wilson was the son, so perhaps it was Ted Wilson's son. That would be the old man's grandson. He owned thousands of sheep. He'd walk all over from Ma'lborough, funny how we always say Ma'lborough. I know it's Marlborough, really, but it's always Ma'lborough to us.

From house-boy in the summer to rabbit-catcher in the winter was quite a change, but I didn't stay there very long, an' then I went to work with dad at the Foundry. There, they had this old pony an' I used to take all the oil an' spares, like plough shares round to all the traction-engines an' threshin' machines. Places like Soley an' Eastridge an' Froxfield an' Bedwyn. Wherever they were workin'. Then, when Osmonds gave up the Foundry I went to work for Ern Watts at Whittonditch. I can especially remember 1921 which was a very hot summer. I was with Sam Gaskin. We was cuttin' a swathe round a corn field ready for the binder an' Sam took his shirt off! In those days, nobody took his shirt off! O'course now you see people with nothin' on an' take no notice! In those days it didn't matter what the farm worker was doin', he never took his shirt off! It must have been hot! Sam was cuttin' the corn with a scythe an' I was tyin' it up in sheaves. This was in a field right opposite Tommy Trots at Whittonditch. It was hot! Sam sent me down two or three times to Trot's Farm to get bottles of water."

BEES, POSTMEN AND VILLAGE FOLK

Gordon

"It was a healthy life but there were often small problems, an' these often gave rise to sayin's, like my mother used to say 'I'm full of aches an' pains that nobody dies of!' Another thing she used to say if she was a bit upset was 'It's enough to make you go up an' never come down anymore!' Then there's that one that Mary uses, 'If you live with cripples, you'll learn to limp!'.

Mother used to get neuralgia. She used to get a bad head, an' one day she got bees in her bonnet. There was a thatched house at the bottom of the garden where the Whitings used to live. Now this would be when I was quite small. Tommy Whiting, who lived there, kept bees. Well, Rumball's cows came from the next meadow an' got into the garden, an' mother an' one or two of the other women went round to drive these cows out. There was nobody there, I think that Tommy Whiting an' the rest of them had gone to work. These cows knocked a beehive over! O'course the bees flew out an' mother got a lot of bees in her hair! The other women had awful trouble gettin' the bees untangled!

My mother was full of sayings an' poetry. One I think she taught me was called 'How the Forget-me-not got its name.' I think I can remember it. It goes ...

When to the flowers so beautiful
The Father gave the names,
Back came the little blue-eyed one,
So timidly it came,
And looking in The Father's face
It said in tones of love and grace,
'Father, the name thou gavest me,
Alas I have forgot,'
Kindly The Father looked him down and said,
'My Child, Forget-me-not.'

Then she had one called 'The Violet'.

Down in a green and shady lane a modest violet grew
Its stalk was bent, it hung its head,
As if to hide from you.
But yet it was a lovely flower,
Its colours rich and rare
It might have graced a rosier bower
Instead of hiding there.

Then there's two lines I can't remember but it finishes,

Then let me to the valley go,
This pretty flower to see
That I may, Oh so long to grow
In sweet humility.

Then dad knew one or two. I can remember his 'Toast'.

> Here's to the man who lies, swears, steals and deceives.
> Lies with his wife, swears to the truth, steals from all
> bad company and deceives the devil!

Then there was a gruesome one!

> Whenever you see a hearse go by,
> You think of the time you're going to die.
> They wrap you up in a big white sheet
> And bury you down about six feet deep.
> All goes well for about a week
> And then the coffin begins to leak.
> The worms crawl in and the worms crawl out,
> They crawl in thin and they crawl out stout.
> One little worm, who is not so shy,
> Crawls into your ear and out of your eye.
> Your hair drops out and your teeth turn green
> And your brains come out like curdled cream!

And thats old! There's nothin' new about horror comics!

Let's talk about something different! I can remember when the postman used to bring the mail to the village in a two-wheeled box gig painted red with the Royal Monogram on it. He used to come from Aldbourne, down by *The Crown*, then down Oxford Street to the Post Office. Then he used to stable at *The Castle*, that is *The Windsor Castle* pub, overnight. That is round the back, nearly in Back Lane. Then he used to collect the letters an' go off again the next mornin' to Hungerford an' then back again to Lambourn. There may have been another mailcart that may have come out from Ma'lborough, but I can only remember this one. Letters would be delivered to the houses from Ramsbury Post Office an' to all the outlying places as far as Park, all round Park Farm Cottages an' all round there. One village postman was Tommy Lewington, an' the other was Jim Watts who lived at the bottom of the Lane, down at the Knapp. He did it for years. Tommy Lewington was a one-armed man. How he lost his arm I don't know, I was quite small, and a thing like that wouldn't have registered.

One postman did a circle one side of the village an' the other did a similar one the other side. They had a uniform. I can't quite remember the hat, I think it was a flat topped shako, but they probably didn't wear it much. One of them used to bring home snake skins, that grass snakes had shed, an' hang them up outside his back door. Tommy Lewington was a very nice man.

Then there was another mysterious chap in the village made up rhymes, mostly all the people in the village band and others but all of the people he wrote about were Primitive Methodists.

There was one that went

> There was old Jane Bull with her go-cart,
> Follows the band from daylight to dark.

And of course the rude ones,

> There's old Bill with his blue glasses
> Pokes his nose up other folks' arses.

And,

At the word of command the band arose,
To see 'Cowy' Chamberlain pickin' his nose.

Then,

Frank Hunter, up the Hill livin'
Wears his trousers a'tater diggin'!

Sid reminded me of some of those! They are obviously the only ones we can remember. I don't know who they were made up by ... I don't think it was 'Monster'..."

Olive

"Who did you call 'Monster'?"

Gordon

"Jack Barnard. We called him 'Monster' because he was small. His brother Frank lived down Blind Lane, just below Mount Pleasant in those houses on the right. He married the ginger-haired girl, Gladys Hunter. The Barnard's mother wasn't married but she had eight or nine children an' they were all on the small side, but she looked after them, they were always tidy and well-dressed. A credit to her really. But 'Monster' used to make up some of the rhymes, I feel sure. There's one I remember about a girl who was seduced by the mailcart driver ...

Have you heard about our Beat?
She's had a nipper!
As fat an' as plump as a kipper!

The 'Monster' once said that Beat was round Back Lane talking to Mrs Bellington (well her name was Allington but the 'Monster' used to call her Bellington) an' she says to her, 'What a bonny little chap! What do 'e fee 'un on?' An' she said 'Only boiled bread an' breast ma'am!'

They were the Allingtons, an' the Prime Minister that was, Lord Home he is now, married one of the Allingtons that lived at the Rookery. That was the house opposite the Church Hall."

Olive

"That was where I said the Wyndhams lived! That must have been after. The lane that goes up to the top is called Orchard Close. There used to be the football pitch, then there was council houses. Margery Giddings, Punch's daughter, lived up there. Anyway, Joan Wyndham has just written a book, it's called *'Love Lessons'* I think. She starts the book off with the words 'Orchard Close, Ramsbury.' An' it's all about her love life during the Second World War!"

Gordon

"Orchard Close is up behind the school. Standing with your back to Shepherd's, the bakers, you go past the school an' turn right, then right again. The Rookery had big iron gates. Then the Hyde-Parkers lived beyond Burdett Street at Badorgan House. Talkin' about Badorgan there used to be a little footpath opposite that used to go up into the allotments that they called Knowledge, where it's all built up now. Old Hopper Tucker who lived down Burdett Street had an allotment an' we boys used to go down to him in the summer an' stand outside *The Burdett Arms*, perhaps seven or eight of us, an' he would tell us yarns.

One night, when it had been a pretty wet season he said 'Aint the slugs been terrible this year? Do you know, the other night I was goin' up to Knowledge Allotments, goin' up to the stile at the top, when I heard this poppin' an' crackin' an' I thought, I wonder what's up now? Well, when I got down to my allotment would you believe this? They damn slugs had het the runner beans goin' up', he said, 'an' they were eatin' the sticks comin' down! I think I'll take a bit of salt up tomorrow night, 'cause I don't want them to get indigestion!'

Another time Hopper said 'Now I'm very fond of cucumber, but the trouble is that if you cut a cucumber tonight, by tomorrow night it's gone a bit stale. So, I'll tell you what I've done. Our kitchen is along like that. I sits here an' the missus sits across there' he said, 'so what I've done is that I've knocked a hole in the brick wall, an' I've put a drainpipe in there through into the kitchen, an' I've grown the cucumbers just outside', he said, 'then when the cucumbers start to grow I just push one up the pipe, then all I got to do when I'm sittin' havin' me tea', he said 'is cut a lump off. An' the next night there'll be another bit through! An' all fresh,' he said. 'All still growin' on the plant! Then you know those new sort of potatoes', he said, 'don't they grow big! I put some in my garden, an' you might not believe this, but there was more in the other bloke's garden, than there was in mine!'

He was a great storyteller, old Hopper Tucker, I don't suppose you remember him?"

Olive

"I remember the name, but why was he called 'Hopper'?"

Gordon

"He limped. An' he had a son with a clubbed foot, but Hopper used to keep us boys amused for hours telling us these yarns which he made up as he went along. We were a good audience, gullible! An' we'd nothin' else much to do really. He'd got no money, neither had we, so we just stood at the corner an' talked."

THE FOUNDRY AND MORE GAME

Gordon

"It was in Kent that I first drove a car. I never had a chance to drive in Wiltshire, hardly to sit in one. Very few people had cars, I mean, Gores, who were big farmers, didn't have a car, they had a pony an' trap. One of the brothers had a motorbike, a Douglas flat twin. He came to the foundry for quite a long time when father was there. I think after Osmond died an' Wilson bought the foundry he came there an' sort of supervised it. It was Wilson the farmer who bought it.

There were three sets of steam ploughs, three or four traction engines an' threshers, two or three chaff cutters, the big ones that went on the end of the threshing machines. Then there was a road engine with rubber strakes on the back they used to do the road work with; like going into the station with trucks an' things. Wilson bought all that as a going concern, but the mouldin' was stopped. Then Wilson had another blacksmith's shop at Axford Farm. Dad used to walk there an' work with him.

Before Gores had the farm at Knighton the Hosiers had it. That was the man who invented the portable milking bail. He was always inventin' something, but that was after he moved out on to the downs. I used to lead his horses every summertime when I was only a little kid! He always used to wear a bowler hat. When Hosier went to Knighton the old boys in the village swore that he'd spoil the farm. He was the first man to use any quantity of artificial manure. The ol' chaps said that the farm would be spoilt in three or four years, but whether it was or whether it wasn't I don't know, but he used to grow some terrific crops there. It was at Knighton Farm when Hosier was there that I first saw a steam Gyrotiller workin'. It went down a terrific depth an' stirred up the soil. I went to school with his son ...I believe it was Ben Hosier. His father's name was Joshua."

Olive

"Wasn't Dad given the sack from the foundry? By some young bloke who took over? I might have got the story wrong, but he was told that he was too old and he had to go on the dole! Of course, that was before he was sixty-five."

Gordon

"That must have been Ted Wilson."

Olive

"That was before he got the Old Age Pension. They always sent somebody round to find out what your position was. You know, how many children? Whether they were workin', whether they would pay you money to help you to live. They wanted to know who I was an' Mum said that I was her daughter's child. And so they said, 'She can pay something towards the child's keep an' they arranged that my mother should pay a half a crown a week to keep me! But at that time, because we only had about ten bob a week to live on, we could only buy the bare essentials. One Saturday when I went up to get the groceries, with only just a short list of things we had to have, Mum didn't have enough money to send and she told me to ask him if we could have it today and we'd pay for it next week. George Rosier's son, Tony, was behind the counter but he wouldn't let me have it! I was only a little kid but I went back down and told Mum. Then somehow she managed to rake up a few shillings and I went down to Vokins' instead, down the street. I'll never forget that. But my mother did help clothe me. I used to go to Swindon, where she lived, every Easter holiday and again during the summer holiday and my mother used to fit me out with a summer outfit and a winter outfit. When I came back from Swindon, Doris used to come down to the end of the court to see me get off the bus! I always had new clothes on and Doris would always burst out crying!"

Gordon

"Oh, she'd cry at anything."

Olive

"I'll always remember I was sent an emerald hat and coat, and it was too big, but the coat was turned up and as I grew, so the hem was let down."

Gordon

"How they brought up such large families in such small houses with so little money was a work of art. Whenever I got a new jacket, well, it wasn't often new, the first thing I did was to slit the lining to put a rabbit in! I could never go anywhere without looking for a rabbit or a fish or eggs, never! So I had to have my jacket like that. An' this carried on until not so many years ago! Even now, if I go alongside a wood, I'm still looking for rabbits! Lots of times Sid an' I would go out for a Sunday afternoon walk and I'd see a rabbit an' I'd pick up a stone, well we always pick up two stones, an' I'd 'heft' them. Well, that's what we called it in Wiltshire ... they'd just have to fit me hand. I always picked up two. If you threw the first one an' you missed, you always had another one to throw.

Before the war, there were so many keepers you had to be careful. I think that at Littlecote there were nine or ten keepers. The head keeper lived just over the water at the Weir, that's what we called it, that's down at Chamberlain's end. During the 14-18 war, when we used to go beatin' they used to give us dinner there. The people at Littlecote then were called Leybourne-Popham an' I remember her sayin' she was goin' to feed seventy people without a coupon! She fed us venison an' rabbit! The keepers' cottages were spread out over the estate so that they could keep an eye on their beats. If you worked on a farm an' you went across a field on a Sunday an' the keeper spied you through his telescope, you'd be on the carpet on Monday morning to explain what you were doing! It was terrible, really. They used to carry on about the damage that rabbits done, an' there was so many about, but they wouldn't let you catch a rabbit, well, not legally! That was a terrible crime! If they caught you they nearly sent you to clink!

When I worked for Willy Hobbs the shoot came under Crowood Estate. It was Giddins'. They had a keeper there that started rearin' the game. Not the one that nearly caught us when Sid an' I went poachin', they had another keeper then but I can't think of his name. But one day we were ploughin' in a field just up to the left of Crowood Lane when a lot of these young pheasants came along the hedge at the top end. I couldn't resist it! I knew I shouldn't do it but when I got to the top an' the horses were turnin', I picked up a stone ... an' Bang! Over one went! So I puts it in me pocket, well, in the linin' an' when I turns the next time. Lo an' Behold! There was the keeper an' his dog an' he's talkin' to the carter! So I stopped there, well, I had to 'cause if I'd had turned an' gone straight away he'd have thought there was something funny. So I stopped! An' do you know, that dog never smelt the pheasant! An' I was afraid all the time he was goin' to! I mean, I couldn't have said I'd run over the pheasant with a plough!"

Olive

"When we lived at Littlecote Park Farm after the war most of the chaps used to catch rabbits and game to eke out their low wages. The German prisoners of war, who lived in the house next door, would put out rabbit wires for pheasants, especially Alois Hotz and Bernard Dobrowski and Freddy and Charlie, who lived in the wooden bungalow and were supposed to be diddykais from Romsey, used catapults, particularly when they went in the woods cutting thatching spars. Most of the game was taken to the thatcher in the village after dark. He was a part-time dealer and had some sort of outlet, I suppose."

Gordon

"When I worked at the foundry with me dad they had a little meadow where they used to turn the ol' pony out. A water-meadow it was, down Newtown. Anyway, once when I went down there I saw a pheasant. The first time I'd seen a pheasant down there. You couldn't sort of chase it because it would be gone. There were no stones an' I wondered how I would get it. Well I was settin' a rat-trap one day an' I thought 'That's it!' So I takes a rat-trap down to the field an' I sets it as light as ever I could an' I put a bit of corn on the plate. The next day I goes down an' there's a pheasant in there! I got seven or eight like that! Once they'd gone at the corn they were stone-dead! Eventually, when I went down, the trap an' all was gone! I expect someone had seen it from the road an' took it with the pheasant in it! It was a gin-trap, a rabbit-trap not a rat-trap, 'cause a rat-trap was smaller."

Olive

"I seem to remember that one of the ways most pheasants were caught at Littlecote was by the chaps diving off the tractors an' trailers as they passed by a pheasant trying to take off against the rabbit-wire that went round all the woods. If they were quick enough to stop the tractor they could just about catch them."

Gordon

"That ol' pony I was talkin' about was Osmond's, not Wilson's. I used to take the stuff round to the traction-engines in a spring-cart (that's what they called it) but when the pony got older an' had a job to get up the hills I'd put a sack on his back an' sling two drums, one on either side. That's what I eventually did. Lots of times there was oil for the steam engines, 'cause they oiled the bearings at least once an' often twice a day. Of course there was no other transport an' this ol' pony had to carry whatever was needed. That's all they'd got. As fat as a pig, it was, every time I used to go round to a threshing machine I used to pinch some oats. I always had a sack of oats, an' a sack of wheat as well, if I could! 'Cause Dad could sell that to someone for their chickens see? If the chap on the baggin' was one of the firm I'd say, 'Give us some wheat,' an' he'd put a bushel in a bag!".

CARNIVAL

Gordon

"There was never any drink in the house as a regular thing, couldn't afford it! Mother may have had a glass of stout sometimes an' Dad only had beer. Never any whiskey or stuff like that! Perhaps if Dad was in the money he may have bought her a bottle of stout or something. I think he may have once or twice but other than that nothing, well at least not when I was at home. Neither of us boys drank, we never went to the pub."

Olive

"I think that when Mum was younger Dad used to get her down as far as *The Burdett Arms* on a Carnival night, and she had a drink then. Once a year, but nothing at all when she got older. That was the only time she went down that street."

Gordon

"The Carnival Week in Ramsbury was really good. It was the highlight of the year, really. You had something every night of the week. You started off with a Service up the Rosier's field. On the Monday you had Whist Drives, on Tuesday, something else."

Olive

"Tuesday we had Penny Trail. All the pennies laid out up the street and at every shilling we'd put a mark. We did one up High Street and another up Oxford Street and our lot used to try and get more with flags and bunting. They used to have strings or ropes tied along the houses in the High Street, up Oxford Street and down Blind Lane, and hung on these strings used to be jam-jars which they painted and they put lighted candles in. (She laughs) that was the fairy lights! It used to look nice though!"

Gordon

"I think it was wires, not strings, that they hung the jam-jars on but I agree with you, they did look nice all painted up. They weren't any danger to the thatched roofs, they were too low for that. Talkin' about thatch, we used to go down the street in the winter an' look up at the holes in the thatch an' see the sparrows pokin' their heads out. But the Carnival! That was really smashin'! I know one year they raised two hundred an' thirty four pounds. All those years ago! I mean, for a little village!

A farmin' community where there was no money ...two hundred an' thirty four pounds for the hospital!"

Olive

"There was a Fancy Dress Competition. There was always great fun in deciding what to go as ... when I was dressed up Dad used to raise some money by taking me round the pubs and standing me on the bar! One year I went as Wilfred the Rabbit, the one that used to be a newspaper cartoon at that time. I think it was called 'Pip, Squeak and Wilfred'."

Gordon

"After I left Ramsbury, I went back home one year at Carnival time an' a boy I used to go to school with said, 'Shall we go in the Carnival?' I agreed an' he said 'What shall we go as?' I said, 'I don't know'.

Then suddenly I said, 'I've got it!'"

We got a perambulator an' we got about four dollies an' put in this pram, an' I dressed up as a lady an' he dressed, which he was, as a man, an' we had a placard on the front which said, 'What Daddy Done in the Great War!'

Then there was Punch Giddings. He was the life and soul of the village, Punch was, an' he went as Ghandi! He went in a white sheet! An' every now an' then he pulled his skirt up an' he'd got a bloomin' great potato there!

Boy Chamberlain, him an' somebody else dressed up an' went in an old tourin' Austin Seven. They put a bed on top an' they went as the Reverend Davidson of Stiffkey. One of them dressed up as a chorus girl or prostitute or whatever it was, an' they were collectin' money in a chamber pot! They collected a hell of a lot of money!

It was mostly horse-drawn floats or with somebody pullin' them. Dad went in once with ol' Bill Watts an' they had bellows on an' an anvil. They had everything on that wagon, they made horse shoes goin' round the village. Father holdin' the iron an' three people strikin' for him. It must have taken a bit of doin' on the move!

At the August Bank Holiday Flower Show the Sports were in the afternoon. They had every sport you could think of! They had runnin', the greasy pole, pillow fightin' horse trottin', horse racin', although there wasn't all that many ridin' horses about in those days. Sid Watts had a lot and he'd lend them to anybody. That's where most of them came from.

It was a really good afternoon. They had a race for the 'Over-Forties' ... I can remember Dad running in it! I remember him takin' his boots off! I thought ... 'I wonder why he's takin' his boots off?' ... I think he came in about third, so he didn't do too bad. I never entered any races, I know, but I had a lot of fun.

The Flower Show was really something for a village. Everybody, more or less, entered something or the other, it wasn't the fact that there was a few prizes, it was the honour of doing it. Just to see who could grow the biggest or the best potatoes. The only time I entered was when I didn't know anything about it!"

Olive

"Sid used to enter a lot! He put a lot of flowers in! Gloxinias were his speciality then, he used to grow them at home, at Mount Pleasant, but sometimes there was cattiness an' I remember someone saying that he grew them at the Manor where he worked."

Gordon

"Then at night, on the same day, they had a dance at the Memorial Hall. I never did any dancin', the only dancin' I did was to plough furrows! I remember going' to a dance an' tryin' to dance once, with Gladys Wootton when she was much younger an' much slimmer than she was the last time I saw her. I trod on her foot an' she said, 'You trod on my foot!' An' I thought, 'That's the last time I dance with anybody!' An' I never danced with anybody else again! I was so disgusted with meself that I couldn't do a simple step like that! I never went anymore. Well, that's a lie! I used to go an' stand at the door as most of the boys did.

At the Memorial Hall they had little shows, films, vaudeville shows an' suchlike. It was sixpence to go in an' they often had some girls in tights, an' I remember one of the farmers sayin' to another, 'What are you doin' here?' an' the other one said, 'I've come to have me sixpennyworth of leg mate!' I mean, in a country place you didn't see many girls in bikinis! I don't say they were good turns but they gave the village people a laugh!

But the shows I remember most was when Tom Pullen had his films over the top of his shop in The Square. He had a cinema show there once a week. If they took too long to put the next film on they used to shout out 'Ring the bell, Sammy!'. There was a boy named Sammy Newman who rang the bell when the programme was going to start. If they got fed-up with waiting they shouted out 'Ring the bell, Sammy!'".

The Square with the Ramsbury tree
c1920s.

German P.O.W.s at
Littlecote Park.

Ramsbury tree in summer
c1910.

MONEY FROM THE HORSES

Gordon

"Harrison's the haberdashers used to supply all the village an' all the way round with stuff. People sent their orders in. Sidney Watts, who hired out horses and vehicles, would provide a pony or a horse and cart an' one of the boys used to go round to Harrison's, collect all the parcels that had been ordered an' take them all around the village an' the outskirts of the village an' collect any orders for next week. That was a regular weekly one. One time you went over Bedwyn side of the village an' the next time you went over the other way. Sid Watts always had plenty of schoolboys helping in the yard and, of course, all of the boys wanted to get the Harrison's job!

Two boys usually went an' this old gig thing used to be loaded up with parcels, all done up, all labelled. All the boys wanted to get on that job, 'cause there was always something from everybody you went to, an apple or a penny, so naturally everybody had to try an' get the job if they could. Sidney Watts in those days had thirty ponies an' the buggys were beautifully kept. All varnished up! People used to hire them the same as you hire a car now. He used to have the order book with all the orders in, some to go to Hungerford, some to go to Ma'lborough, and you could drive yourself or have somebody to drive you. It was quite a business.

There was always a lot of competition to be taken on at Sid Watts' yard. But it wasn't just Sid Watts you had to satisfy. Oh no! There was a sort of initiation ceremony carried out by the regulars and led by the "head boy". In my time, that was Arthur Talmadge.

What happened was this.

When Sid Watts was out of the way, the new lad, surrounded by all the others would be led to old Topsy's stall. Now Topsy was a quiet old mare tied up right at the end. The new boy would be stood facing the mare's tail which the head boy would lift. Then without more ado the other lads would grab the new boy by the scruff of the neck and ram his face right into old Topsy's behind! What's more, they made sure that his face was well an' truly scrubbed round in whatever there was there! What old Topsy must have thought, I really don't know! Of course, it was only schoolboy fun, but if you didn't pass the test, you had no chance of getting any money from the horses!

On Saturday nights he checked up the takin's. I can see him now sittin' on the corn bin with all the boys round an' him goin' through the order book. Who did this one? Who did that one? An' then he'd give us the money. He'd give the little ones a tanner each, the bigger boys perhaps a shilling! None of them really worked for him, they were all part-time.

Sid an' Ern Watts were Bill Watts the blacksmith's sons. Sid Watts kept his ponies at the bottom of Blind Lane by the blacksmith's shop. Ernest was the eldest but he never made much of a go of it. He had the farm at Witcha. They said that some of them lost quite a lot of money through gamblin'. Ern Watts an' Roger Chamberlain an' several more of them used to play at the Ramsbury Building Society offices. They used to go down there nights, an' I don't know if Ern Watts lost any of his money there but anyway he gave up the farm. Now Sydney was the opposite. He started up with a couple or three old donkeys an' he finished up with a couple or three farms! By the way, I think that Roger Chamberlain was the Boy Chamberlain's father."

CHOIR PRACTICE AND MORE VILLAGE FOLK

Gordon

"I don't remember too much about the Memorial Hall, mostly about the Church Hall an' the Wesleyan Chapel where I belonged to the concert party. I remember goin' out to Vernham Dean once in an' old char-a-banc. I always used to say a monologue of various sorts. If it wasn't one of Charlie Sparrow's it would be one that I'd bought for about three pence from a list of titles that I'd sent away for. The Day family used to be in it, all the boys an' two of the girls. Although I was in the Wesleyan Concert Party, I also sang in the Church Choir with Sid, my brother. The Reverend Shuttleworth was the rector. He was the short one an' he gave me a reference when I left Ramsbury. I can't remember which came first but anyway, me an' a boy I went to school with named Alec Russell, who left Ramsbury before I did, an' went to Epsom, or somewhere, all during the winter we went round the chapels, we went to the Wesleyans one Sunday, the Primitives the next, then the Methodists, the Church an' the Salvation Army, an' when we'd finished, we went back round again. An' we did that all the winter! We just did it because we liked it. We liked to go to the Salvation Army especially, we used to get up the back an' sing as loud as ever we could! An' then they'd say, 'Would we come up to the front an' be saved!'"

Olive

"Gladys went to the Salvation Army one year when I was there! 'Would she like to be saved!' I was only a kid an' I didn't know what was going on!"

Gordon

"Quite a lot of people used to go up an' be saved! Just for a fortnight or three weeks!"

Olive

"Some of the village children used to go to each chapel for two or three Sundays before it was time for their outing, just so that they could go with each trip!"

Gordon

"It was on an outin' that it was the first time I ever saw the sea. I should imagine I was about seventeen then. Anyway, there was a man named Jones an' he lived up Union Street. I became quite friendly with him but I don't know why I did because I didn't really know him very well, but anyway, he said to me, 'Have you ever been to the seaside Gordon?' 'No,' I said, 'I've never seen the sea'. 'Would you like to go?' he said, an' I said 'Yes!' So he said, 'I belong to the Church Choir' an' he said, 'I'll take you an' I'll pay the money.'

We went to Weston-super-Mare an' I remember they had to have two engines to pull us up one part! An' when we got to the top, he said, 'Look there Gordon, there's the sea!' An' I said, 'No it's not, that's clouds all along there! That's blue sky!' An' he said, 'No that's the sea.' An' that's the first time I'd seen the sea. We went into Weston-super-Mare an' I bought mother a little brooch for about a shilling. An' that was all through the goodness of this man Jones. I can't think of his other name, his father was a bootmaker down at the other end of the village. I don't know where he worked but I think he had a bit of ground at the back of our houses. Now he was the first person I ever saw using a Dutch hoe. Nobody in Ramsbury used a Dutch hoe in those days, they either had a draw hoe or what's called a peewit hoe. A peewit hoe was a frame hoe. A draw hoe is a swan-neck hoe an' a peewit hoe has a loose blade. You can make the blade any width you like from pieces from an old saw blade. Then, if you make the blade shallow, drawing all the dirt towards you, some went over the frame. That way the ground was pretty clean an' you could hoe nine or ten inches at once! But a peewit hoe was probably a Wiltshire name. There were other names too, an' a fork, a hay fork was always a two-grained prong. An' a four grained prong would be a dung fork."

Olive

"Gordon, can you remember Dad making an aerial ropeway at the Manor? Sid has some memories of it."

Gordon

"I was still at school. But I think it was for some fete, but that was the first time I'd rowed a boat. When father was putting up that ropeway at Manor Farm, I went down to the boat-house. There was a canoe with a double scull, an' I got in an' I sculled out around that lake. I didn't think about it then but I couldn't swim! I wonder what would have happened if I'd have fell out? An' I'll tell you what I found in the water in the boathouse! A mug of the Coronation of George an' Mary! The water was clear, nobody had been in there. We had that mug at home for years. The ropeway just went from one tree to another with a pulley wheel. You just hung onto the wheel at one end an' shot down the rope to the other an' just stopped yourself with your feet up against a mattress. That was the time when Ernest Watts sent me to be ball-boy for the tennis tournament and' I bought a pot of jam an' a pair of breeches!"

Olive

"Sid can also remember Dad making a barbeque at the foundry which they used to roast an ox on the frozen lake at Ramsbury Manor. Were you there then Gordon?"

Gordon

"I can remember something about it but it must have been after I left. But I can remember the river down the bottom of the Lane, where you used to drive the cows in to drink, all freezin' over an' Roger Chamberlain ridin' his horse on the ice.

An' that reminds me. Do you remember Garnet Rosier? Well he used to bring the cows down the Lane, didn't he? Down to drink at the bottom. Now he was deaf an' dumb. An' those cows used to go right out into the stream. Now, how did he get them out? He was deaf an' dumb, but he got them out alright with no trouble at all! They seemed to know what he meant when he made these funny noises. I used to go about with him quite a lot. I used to go down with him to the field where he used to keep the cows at Crowood. He was always doin' signs to me. Sometimes I could understand what he meant an' sometimes I couldn't. He was one of the Rosier family. He had two sisters. One suffered from goitre, one ... was Katie ..."

Olive

"She used to dish up the milk at the back door of the shop, then there was George an' Len Rosier, the brothers."

Gordon

"John Rosier kept the grocers. They'd been there for years, then, when he went, Len Rosier took it on an' then Tony. He was the nephew, wasn't he? George Rosier's son. He took it over. I tell you what Olive! Do you remember Roland Reed? He used to have the shop that belonged to Vokins didn't he? They used to make beautiful bread. I remember goin' in there once and Roland Reed was there an' they'd got a piece of corned beef on the counter that they used to cut bits off. Well there was a loose bit there an' Roland picked it up an' put it in his mouth! I don't suppose he ever thought twice about it! But I remember!

Then there was a Chamberlain who was a bootmaker down at the other end of the village. There was lots of Chamberlains, two were carriers. There was George Chamberlain an' Jack Chamberlain who lived round Back Lane. They'd be horse carriers. They had a thickish cob an' they used to sell coal. One day a week they went into Hungerford an' Ma'lborough, an' they took a few people in. Some of the carriers had covered wagons. Mabel Denton, that become Mrs Westall, had one before she had a car, an' that first car she had was an' old American Essex. Once when I went home I went into Ma'lborough with her in this Essex an' the bloomin' thing! Every time she went to start it, it wouldn't! I managed to get it goin' an' I drove it all the way through Ramsbury stoppin' to deliver the parcels. A little one here an' a little one there. That was the first car she had, but before that they had a horse an' cart. Mabel Denton was her name before she was married. Her husband had a nickname, but I can't remember what it was, but I know she had a son we called 'Cocker'. It was rather a mixed-up lot. The Chamberlains were a very big family. There was the woodman who lived over the water at Lamplands at the bottom of Spring Hill. I went to work for him for two or three weeks, when I hadn't got a job. An' he used to go up into the woods that belonged to Littlecote an' collect wood for sawin' up for logs with this flat-bottomed trolley. Before we started, I used to get a pocket full of stones to throw at all the pheasants on the way. I remember we got up to Rudge Farm. There'd been an old cornstack an' there was all these pheasants! An' I stood up on this trolley an' I threw this stone an' it killed this bloomin' pheasant! Of course, I jumped down an' got it but it frightened the woodman out of his life! He was afraid that the keeper would think that it was him! 'Cause he was gettin' the wood from Littlecote! He didn't mind me killin' it but he was afraid that he'd get the blame!

He was a funny chap, I remember one day his horse bit him an' he got hold of the horse's lip an' he bit him as well! An' he said, 'There you are, you B, that'll larn yer!' He was a case! But he was a nice old boy. He was called 'Boshy' Chamberlain. I don't know what 'Boshy' was supposed to mean, but his sons were called Frankie Bosh, Freddie Bosh an' Sammy Bosh. They called them all that name although their name was Chamberlain!

Another time I worked for Bert Wootton. They grew watercress. Bert had two or three old ponies. He had a stable up Crowood Lane. I had a fat old pony an' an old costermonger's cart, an' each day I'd have to go round to the meadow, to the beds they were cuttin', and load the watercress an' take it to Hungerford Station. It was all cultivated. With all that water about there was plenty of osiers an' at one time there were quite a few basket makers. I remember there was one at Axford I think he made the watercress baskets. They were very coarsely made and they held about half hundredweight each. There was so many "hands" of cress in each basket. These Woottons were big chaps with big hands an' you'd be surprised how much cress they could hold in one hand. The "hands" were never tied at all but were laid in the baskets just so. They never moved once they were in. At a place like Harbrook the beds were quite a way from where the old pony could get so they used to chuck the baskets in the river an' they used to float down! When they got them out the other end they ran with water! But they had oil skins to carry them. They were often sopping wet through. They stood in the water to cut the cress an' they had waders. They always walked home in them. You could always hear the Woottons even if you couldn't see them! Bert Wootton used to put the cress up into small "hands" and take it to Swindon.

The watercress beds were all about the same size although it was governed a bit by the amount of water that was coming up. They had a proper drilling rig to put the pipes down to the water table an' the water used to just come up the pipes like a spring. There be no pumps or nothing of that! Just natural pressure. It was all clean, pure water except where the ducks an' moorhens went through. They used to give them trouble when the new beds were growin' an' they tried all manner of things to keep them out. That was one of the bugbears. The ducks wavered about here an' there, all over the place, an' spoilt quite a lot.

Dad used to help them drill these pipes sometimes. Each bed had got a pipe of fresh water comin' down all the time all kept at the same level. These were at Harbrook. They had them down Newtown an' they had another one somewhere else. The main part of the watercress always went to Birmingham. None ever went to London. I wasn't there very long, I fell out with him. Bert was about my age an' one mornin' he told me I was late an' I said I wasn't an' I told him he could keep his job! An' I just walked out.

There was watercress beds at Axford where Sid lived. Stocker Wootton's brother used to go over there to see them. It was Stocker Wootton who was the man I used to go drovin' with. He used to work for George Wilson. An' he would do the drovin'. He'd got this old milk-float with this ol' pony named 'Dodger', an he would go out about ten miles, say the other side of Ma'lborough an' collect perhaps twenty or thirty cattle, or a couple of hundred sheep, an' we would bring them home. An' my job, when we went through the towns, was to run along in front an' shut the gates up. They were all driven along the road in those days. So I used to go in the front an' shut the gates up an' the dog used to do the rest.

In the old country lanes we'd get up in the float an' let the dog do all the work. Hundred head was nothing really! 'Cause there was no traffic to worry about. In the town an odd car but nothin' much.

He used to take with him a bottle of drink called "bee" wine. It was a sort of mead made from the old drained honey combs. Almost everybody in Ramsbury had a bottle fermentin', takin' some out an' puttin' some more water in. I suppose it was like a ginger beer plant. It got quite heady! When it was warm an' I'd had half a dozen drinks of this bee wine I didn't care whether these sheep went into anybody's garden or whether they didn't!

Stocker Wootton was John Wootton's brother. He lived down Newtown. There was another brother who lived up Blind Lane. I can't think of his name, but he was a shepherd. They were a family of big men. John Wootton lived up in the council houses. His wife never referred to him as 'my husband' or 'Mister Wootton', she always spoke of him as 'John Wootton'.

John Wootton was the water bailiff. He used to be down on us boys like a ton of bricks if he thought we was after moorhens' eggs, which we always were. If he hadn't cured us a bit we'd have become like some of these unruly young folk are today!

As far as fish was concerned we really only went after trout. We didn't have the tackle to go after anything in deep water. When the trout got in the narrow streams, two of us boys would stand about twenty yards apart on opposite banks an' drive the fish backwards an' forwards. Eventually the fish would lie flat on the bottom. An' then we used to snare them. That's get them with a snare on a stick. We used catapults mostly when they were scoopin' out the bed, which they did by movin' their bodies backwards an' forwards, they moved quite big stones an' they was easy meat! They'd never be more than ten yards away! Then when you'd hit them with a stone you could nip in an' fetch them!

But the snare was a good idea. You could carry it in your pocket without anyone knowin'! Of course with all these willows about there was always plenty of sticks to tie the snare on but it wasn't everybody who could snare them. You had to have the know-how! You had to guide the snare over them carefully. If you touched them with it before you were ready they went! I know that lookin' at those sort of things through the water makes it more difficult but we could do it quite easily. You moved the wire down to about the end of their fins an' give it a snatch an' swing them out on the end of the stick ... if there was nobody about!

We never set snares for pheasants but sometimes if we put a snare in a fence for a rabbit we'd get a pheasant. Neither did we put wires up for deer although some did. Once when I went with Sid up to Hen's Wood there was a deer that had tried to jump a wire cattle fence an' it had got one of its legs trapped in it an' it had just hung up there until it had died.

Terrible!

There was another family I've just remembered. The Smythes. They lived in the farmhouse in Oxford Street. Herbert Smythe. His two boys grew up there. One was Vic Smythe, he was a horse trainer at Epsom. After they had left the village they always used to give the old folks a dinner and packets of tea at Christmas.

The people in the big houses always took an interest in the village, especially when the 'Tobacco Wills' came to the Manor. At Christmas they had these tickets. You could go up there an' they'd give you a chit, an' then you'd go to the butchers an' the grocers an' get half a crown's worth of what you fancied at each. I can't remember whether the Burdetts did it, but Sir George Wills did it.

When the Wills moved to Littlecote you could do the same there. Half crown's worth wasn't much but it helped you know! But people used to abuse it. They'd send up all their kids, one at a time, to try an' get more chits!

At Ambrose Farm we'd get oranges at Christmas, two if you were lucky! That was the Chamberlains.

At the Giddins' Christmas Party at Crowood, which they gave to all their tenants on the Whittonditch an' Marridge Hill estates an' their employees, you'd hear some of the real old songs from some of the old boys. Songs that you'd never hear anywhere else.

One of them went,

There was Pa! Half undressed,
A lyin' in the gutter with a mangle on his chest!
Right in the middle of the road!

Then there was another one called 'The Village Pump! The Magpie an' the Stump!' Everybody used to try an' do something. There was nothing organised or anything! I remember there was a boy from our Lane who wasn't quite up to it being pestered by the rest to do something. In the end, he started singin' a rather rude song. He didn't know any different, but then, everyone was tryin' to stop him! I suppose it was quite funny really an' once he got started he didn't want to stop.

One of the labourers, Harry Paine, sang a song. His mother used to keep *The Halfway Inn*. Him an' his brother were proper old country chaps.

One of them used to do a lot of mangold hoein' an' somebody said that they saw him one day hoein' in the rain with an umbrella tied to his shoulders! Of course in those days most hoein' was on piece work so if you didn't work you didn't get any money!

Some stories you hear you can't believe.

There was these two chaps who used to cut hay out of the stack, truss it up an' send it up to London. They had a proper press an' made a very good job of it. But this chap Paine used to do some trussin' too but he never had a press, an' what's more he didn't know the proper knot they used to tie them with. So he got on to these two professionals an' asked them how they tied this knot an' they showed him. He could hardly figure it out an' soon forgot. Then later when they saw him he said, 'I've found out how to do that knot! I was in bed last night with me missus an' I told her how it was done!'. So they said, 'Show us how it's done.' So he got some twine an' he did it wrong! So they said, 'You'd better get back to bed with yer missus an' tell her you got it wrong, an' try again!'

When I was at Ramsbury School an' Mr Stubbs was schoolmaster I had a good memory. Whatever it was I learnt it an' I'd write it down straight away before he gave us the dictation. I'd got it all written down long before the rest was halfway through. He knew I did this so he started to alter some of the words in his dictation so that I got it wrong! I could learn things in a short time, I only had to read something through three or four times an' I'd got it! I think most of us was like that! That was our mother! She was good!"

Olive

"There's so many things to recall it's difficult to get it down in the right order.

I remember one day a girl came up to me as we were going home from school and she said that her grandmother had sent her half a crown. How she sent it I don't know ... by post? So we went out spending and she bought one or two things. First some sweets and then a bottle of scent for sixpence which she gave to me.

When I got home I gave the scent to Gladys. I said that this girl had given it to me. The next day, Mr Ludlow called me by his desk and I didn't know what was going on and he said, 'Did you go with this girl to these shops? What did you buy? How much money was spent?'

And that was that for the time being.

The next day Mr Ludlow came into the classroom and he was talking to Chris Winchcombe, my teacher. I was sitting in the front row right in front of Mr Winchcombe's desk. I heard Ludlow say, 'I blame her for taking the stuff!' What this girl had done was to take the money from one of the teacher's purses!

So I had to get the scent back from Gladys! Because Ludlow said 'Bring it in!'

When I heard Ludlow say, 'I blame her for taking the scent', I burst out crying. I'd had nothing to do with the money at all! But she was like that! She was a bit of a liar! Of course she'd eaten the sweets so they couldn't be returned!"

Gordon

"I remember now you come to speak of it. 'Cause Ludlow an' Chris Winchcombe weren't there when I was there, it was John Stubbs an' Mr Reed. Mr Reed was W.V. Reed. William Vines Reed. A most unusual name! A very versatile man he was, he took all the photographs in the village, sent the reports of village news to the Ma'lborough Times an' did the reports of the plays they put on at the Memorial Hall. He also used to give us the old movin' pictures. A very clever man! By the way, you remember I said that Roland Reed took Vokins' shop? Well, Roland was the schoolmaster's son."

Olive

"There was a teacher there called Mrs Davis. She lived at Axford. She used to take the older girls for sewing and because one of the teachers was away she had our class. We had to go into her room and read while the older girls did sewing. When Mrs Davis had to go out of the room she said to my Aunt Doris, who was one of the older girls, 'You tell me if anyone misbehaves while I'm out of the room'.

Of course, me, cocky-like, thought that 'Oh she's my aunt she won't tell on me,' and so I was talking!

Then, damn me, when Mrs Davis came back if she didn't tell her! Oh dear! I went home and told Mum."

Gordon

"There's always something on in a village, I can recall a domestic commotion in Blind Lane that set us buzzing! We were in bed one night an' we heard a commotion over the road, I don't know whether he was throwin' the crockery at her but there was a row."

Olive

"I can remember after one of their sessions one Saturday, they'd been out drinking, they were fighting. Anyway, the next day she had her arm in a sling! Her arm was broken!"

Gordon

"I tell you what I did see him do, he used to drive a proper diddykai's cart, he only had a two-wheeled one but he always had a good pony. Anyway, I remember him once comin' down Blind Lane an' he was blind drunk! This mare was at a stretched gallop, down from Crowood straight across the crossroads, down Blind Lane, an' he tried to turn her into his gateway halfway down!

He tipped the lot over! He was on the floor, but he got up an' got hold of the old mare's tail an' he said, 'Well done old gal!,' an' he stood there holdin' her tail an pattin' her on the back, an' she just stood there an' trembled.

I can see her now. Fancy him tryin' to turn in there at a gallop! When she got there he just yanked her round! He was a rag an' bone man. He needed the cart for his business. I used to sell the rabbit skins an' mole skins to him. The mole skins had to be dried first, I'd peg them on a board. He always treated me quite reasonable, of course perhaps I didn't know the correct price. He always paid up when I took them over. The rabbits we used to skin ordinary. I suppose he used to send them off like they were.

I used to catch a lot of moles at one time with ordinary mole traps. Out in those water meadows you could catch one about every two or three hours if you had time. I didn't trap at certain times each day, I just used to set the trap an' wait for them. Some folk reckon that moles work about every two hours. But what I found was that if you could find a main run, say comin' from one garden to another, you could catch a mole every day! There'd be fifteen or sixteen! All using the same highway. Out in the open fields they were more difficult to catch. They could go here there an' everywhere an' throw up little mole hills all over the place not more than six inches high, p'raps just raised above the ground. Of course, when the runs are shallow you can see them where they break the turf. But if they're deeper, you have to push a stick down, dig out a slot for the trap, an' then set it before the earth falls back in.

Oddly enough you can hardly buy a mole trap now, you can go round a dozen shops before you can find one!"

FARMING

Gordon

"As I said, after I left the foundry I went to work for Ernest Watts who had a farm at Whittonditch. I used to walk to work in the mornin' an' set rabbit snares on the way. I don't know how I got away with it because it was within sight of the farmhouse, an' all! I always thought that they would say something, but they didn't.

Some of the jobs they gave the boys in those days were terrible. One job he put me at was after the corn was cut an' the stubble was about seven or eight inches high. He had a lot of docks in this field an' he sent me up there pulling them up. The ground was hard an' dry and tryin' to pull up these docks took all the skin off me hands. Anyway one day he came up to me an' said, 'I've got a good job for you Gordon,' an' I said, 'What's that then?' An' he said, 'You go home at dinner time, an' afterwards you go up to the Manor'. That was Sir Ernest Wills' then, an' he said, 'they've got a fete on there, well, you go to the tennis court an' be ball boy'.

Well, there's a lot of difference between pullin' up docks an' bein' a ball boy! Well, I went an' they had this tennis tournament an' I suppose I got a few tips an' with the money I bought a jar of strawberry jam for threepence an' a pair of breeches for threepence. Those breeches were real good. They lasted me for donkey's years!

On the farm, it was the boys who always got the blame. If anything went wrong it was the 'old boy'. An' the jobs they put you on! When they were threshin', they'd put you on the cavins which was the worst job of the lot! You had to get all the cavins away an' carry the chaff perhaps twenty or thirty yards to what they called "the chaff coop". Kids were run off their feet. That was threshin' with the old steam engines.

Bert Giddings was with me at Knighton Farm an' what he used to do was to get a rake an' hook the belt off the thresher. Then they had to stop the threshin' machine to put the belt back on again. You see, very often Bert had to do the cavins and the chaff, and he was only a boy like me, but that's 'ow we got a rest!

We used to put wire nettin' all round the ricks to trap the rats an' mice. An' there were some in those days! I reckon you could always tell a good farmer 'cause if he had a few stacks left about March there'd be so many rats an' mice, half the strings on the sheaves would be eaten. There was always loose straw! An' dust! An' mice by the thousand! Every time you lifted a sheaf up there be a nest of ten or twelve mice. Old ones runnin' all over the place! Up your trouser legs an' in your pockets. Some chaps used to tie string round their trousers to stop the mice runnin' up! But some old men who always wore thick cord trousers used to have these proper straps. Yorkers, they were called. Some folks said that these were to stop the mice, but it wasn't that really, it was just to keep their trousers clean. I mean I've only got to walk up the garden on a wet day an' the bottoms of me trousers are dirty! But if trousers are tied round properly they'll keep clean.

These old cord trousers were so thick that they'd nearly stand up on their own! They were the old fashioned sort with a flap in front. Some call them split-falls or ballops but whatever they're called, I know they had a flap there an' it showed everything!

I tell you what we used to do when we were boys, we used to get hold of a full-grown mouse by the tail an' spin it as fast as ever you could, first one way an' then the other. An' it went giddy! An' then put it down. An' it didn't know which way to go! Poor little things! It didn't know whether to run away or stay with you! But when we were threshin' we just put our feet on any mice we found. Of course, some got away but there was always a lot of mice on the farms. When you were threshin' it was nothin' to go home an' find them in your pockets. Everybody hung their jackets up an' often you'd put your hand in your pocket an' there was a mouse in it!

But talkin' about spinnin' a mouse, we used to try the same game with the old hens. We used to put their head under their wing an' swing them round and round!

Then put them down giddy-like!

Then there's a story about Bert Giddings. He lived in one of the cottages at the top of Blind Lane an' you could get from his house through the back garden to his aunt's house, the front of which was just round the corner in Oxford Street, just opposite Rosier's shop. She used to go across the road to get her groceries an' she always carried them back in her apron. She'd get hold of the bottom of her apron an' make a container of it to put the groceries in.

One day, Bert nipped through the back gardens just as his aunt had gone across the road to Rosier's, an' he hid under the table in the parlour. The table was covered with one of those lovely old mohair table cloths with a bobble fringe all the way round, so he was well hid! When she came back from the shop with her groceries in her apron, he grabbed her by the leg an' she let out a scream an' dropped everything on the floor! She was in such a state that she probably didn't see him slip out of her back door, but he went back to his house, out into Blind Lane, round to her front door in Oxford Street an' asked her what was the matter!

I think that she found out eventually an' I think he got a fine old clip round the ear'ole from his mother! Really, he was a nice boy, Bert Giddings. He married a girl named Nora Pike an' both she an' her parents were in the Salvation Army. Bert joined afterwards. The last time I heard of him workin' was when he was drivin' a road roller for Wilts. County Council. His father was a traction engine driver an' he worked at Osmund's at the time my father worked there. His name was George Giddings but he was called "Ramble". I don't know why. Bert had no brothers but he had two sisters an' one was called Phyllis.

It was through Bert Giddings that I come to work at Knighton Farm. He was there before me. I suppose I was out of a job at the time an' he said there was a job there, at Knighton, so he had a word with the farmer an' that's how I started.

So he was a ploughboy with me but he was one step above because of him being there before me. He had the best bike an' plough lines, if he could get 'old of them! There was always an argument as to who would have the best plough lines. I mean, there was a chap named Phillips, now he would be third in command. There was the carter, the under-carter, an' then Phillips. He was a quiet chap an' when he wasn't doin' anything, he would always be curlin' a bit of hair on his for'head with his finger. We boys were always playin' games with him, perhaps because he was so quiet an' didn't say anthing! More than once, when we'd found a dead rabbit we'd hide it in his dinner bag last thing in the afternoon an' he'd carry it all the way home! If not a rabbit then we'd put in a dandy brush! An' if he had new plough lines, we'd pinch his an' give him an old pair.

The farms I worked on were mostly arable. I didn't have much to do with cows, only on one farm. Of course I used to help milk them when we was short, but normally we worked with horses. The biggest farm I worked at was Thomas Gore's at Knighton on the Littlecote Estate. It was about 600 acres. We had seventeen horses there, there were five teams of three. Each of us had three horses an' we used a plough called a Cockshut plough. That was a short plough with levers on your front an' back furrows.

There were two horses spare for cartin' hay, corn for the sheep an' movin' hurdles. Of course all the sheep were penned in those days. We grew kale, an' roots, mostly swedes. Each shepherd had so many sheep an' so many hurdles. He had to carry these hurdles every day an' make a fresh pen. An' he used to make a beautiful job of it. He'd put those hurdles down across in a perfect square.

The swedes threw up long shoots when they were goin' to seed so they used to turn the old harrows upside down so, instead of havin' their tines on the ground they'd turn them over on their back. You had a couple or horses on it an' you took it over the swedes, an' the squares of the harrows, they always had iron harrows in Wiltshire, pulled the swedes out of the ground an' that stopped the rest from goin' to seed. After the sheep had been folded the ground was perfectly flat where the sheep had trod it. It was a beautiful pan an' of course if it was a bit wet it went down well an' you could cut a perfect furrow!

I remember ploughin' with a couple of odd horses. When you first went to a farm they gave you two odd horses. Horses went in rotation. The head carter would have the best ones an' so on down, down to the little old boy! I was always "the little old boy", I was so small. I couldn't hardly get the collar on some horses. I couldn't even reach his bloomin' head, let along get a collar on! But anyway, they gave me a couple of odd horses, Colonel an' Captain. I can remember their names now. Once we were ploughin' a field at the top of Eastridge Hill, an' I suppose it was about a quarter of a mile from one side to the other an' I stuck one mark up under the wood, a bit of paper on a stick, an' with these two old horses I ploughed the straightest furrows I've ever done in me life. These horses had been at it so long that they could see this bit of paper an' they went straight up there.

When I got to the end I stopped an' turned round an' looked back; an' it was as straight as a gun barrel! Beautiful! I used to love ploughin' whatever the weather.

When I was on that farm I did all the markin' out. They ploughed in 'lands' of twenty yards then, well, twenty strides really. Ten strides around to the right you ploughed, which was called a 'frammard', an' then ten round to the left which was called a 'to'hard'. All these lands had to be marked out every twenty strides, and it all had to be finished. What they called 'hemp'. I suppose it meant 'hempty', I don't know, but I only heard it in Wiltshire. So I did all the markin' out an' all the finishes because it was easier to plough straight with two horses than it was with three.

As I say, I loved ploughin' but I liked anything on a farm. I could do anything too! Any job on the threshin' I could do, except for drivin' the engine! But I think I could have driven that if they'd have let me have a go!

But they used to give the boys some hard jobs, like tyin' up sheaves when they were cuttin' the binder swathe. Makin' sheaves with oats only about a foot long wasn't easy. One length of straw wasn't long enough to tie round so you had to learn to join two bits of corn together in such a fashion with the ears of one between the ears of the other so as they wouldn't break.

At Knighton Farm the arable was above the Hungerford road. Along the river were the water meadows where they used to put all the sheep early on. The Woottons used to do all the 'drownin'' or 'flottin'', as they called it; John Wootton, the water bailiff, an' his son. Of course, that's an art in itself. All those meadows had a little ditch at the top an' a bigger ditch at the bottom. One was probably a yard higher than the other so that all the water drained out. They was blocked up every so many yards so that the water they let in from the river spread out evenly over the land. The idea was to get a good growth of early grass.

To cut out the little ditches they had a breast plough, like a two sided hoe, sort of thing, that they pushed with their chest. It had a handle on it about six foot long an' it was as thick as your arm. Quite a biggish bit of timber. The blade was 'L' shaped so that you could cut along one side of the ditch an' half-way across the bottom. They went up one side an' then when they got to the end of the ditch, they turned round an' came back the other way, an' that way they cut the whole lot out! Then they dug out the loose turf with forks an' used it to dam up the ditch every so often. I can't remember how often, you saw it so many times you didn't take any notice. It wasn't dammed completely mind, there would be enough room left in the middle to let enough water go through to the next dam. It worked so that the surplus water ran over the side of the small ditch, an' down across the field to the bottom ditch, an' so it carried on all over the field. That way they got the grass at least a month earlier.

It was a peculiar kind of grass, something like Yorkshire Fog, very soft. It was all mowed by hand, every bit of it! You couldn't get any machines in those meadows! There was usually a gang that started at the beginning of the summer an' they'd do it at so much an acre. There was no stones of course, an' they used to shave it! It was beautiful! It was all mown into swathes, an' then, all the swathes had to be shaken out with forks. That would be the farmer's gang, shakin' all the grass out until it had been made into hay. You couldn't get wagons in so they'd bring in carts, load them an' cart it out. But I'll tell you one thing about that sort of hay - it heated up very quickly. If it wasn't made properly an' put in the stack, it used to go black! Just like tobacco! When it was cut out of the stack with a hay knife you could only go down about two or three inches because it was so hard! It was like rock!

In those days nearly all boys had to go into domestic service or farm work. There was hardly any other jobs. I can only remember one or two boys who went to school with me who were able to do anything else. Eddie Franklin became a clerk in the G.W.R., which was quite surprising because his father owned *The Bell* as well as the butcher's shop. Ted Brown was apprenticed to a carpenter and there was a boy named Bert Wheeler who used to live down Blind Lane, who became a clerk, but other than that, none. It was the same for girls. My sisters, Hilda an' Gladys, had to go into the service. Hilda went away somewhere, she went to London, one time, for a long time. I know mother didn't hear from her very often when she was up there.

On the farms they always had carters an' cowmen. But if there was anything to be done that needed any other sort of a skill, it was always me! Like sowing grass seed with a seed barrow. With a twelve foot seed box across the barrow that job was alright if you were on the level, but if you got on a bit of hilly ground, it was bloomin' hard work! Of course you had to go up an' down the hill to keep the seed box level otherwise the end of the seed barrow would touch the ground an' the fall of the seed pattern wouldn't be the same. Later, when we had tractors, I got the idea of sittin' on the tractor behind the driver, facin' backwards, an' we pulled the seed barrow behind! That way we done the field in no time! Top gear, an' away we went!

Wagons were tricky to handle, I can't remember how old I was but I went out to some fields next door to Knowledge, probably owned by one of the Woolfords, an; they were cartin' corn. It was on a side bank an' I was just wanderin' behind the wagon an' they went to turn to go back down the hill but they put the chain to hold the wagon round the wheel before they turned! From where I was walkin' behind the wagon I suddenly saw one of the wheels come off the ground. I thought 'Cor! that's funny!', but in a flash the whole lot went over! The horse with his legs in the air, the bloke who'd been on the wagon was underneath all the sheaves an' the wagon was all on its side. I, bein' so young, didn't know what was happenin'. But it was just because they were turnin' with the wheel chained. With those old wagons, whether the wheel was tied or not, that sort of thing very often happened, but ususally, you had sense enough to stop your horses before it went over I've seen horses with their legs in the air many a time! It was because of this we always preferred to use carts with ladders instead of wagons. At Knighton they had no wagons! They had flat-bottomed trolleys, four-wheeled trolleys like railway drays but with ladders on. All flat-bottomed! Beautiful little things! They were easy to load on. You hadn't got very far to load up for a start. The only thing was, you needed a decent loader when you were cartin' corn or hay otherwise it was inclined to sway. Once a chap got used to it they were quite easy to load. They were quite light for the horses an' they turned easy. They were much, much more sensible!

They also used what they called 'Scotch Carts' with angled floors. Then there was the old dung carts which you could tilt up a notch at a time so that you could pull the muck out with a drag. In those days all the muck was put in heaps in the field, so many heaps to the acre. Well, they didn't trouble exactly how many to the acre but that's how it was done. The carter had a drag. That was like a four tined prong with the tines bent at right angles. I can remember doin' that in the First World War. I could only have been about thirteen. I used to have two trace horses besides the one in the cart. I used to drive it up to the chap in the field an' he used to pull it out of the back. Can you imagine a boy of thirteen doin' that now? I was still at school, but they let you off school the last year of the war. If a farmer wanted you, you could go an' work for him see? I always used to get some farmer to take me so as I missed school. I was quite good at school but I got out of it if I could! But you imagine a boy of thirteen drivin' three horses through these gateways! Very often I hit the gatepost! If you were on a bit of a bend the leadin' trace horse was comin' round before the one in the shafts was through the gateway! Oh, I knocked a few gateposts down!

When I did that sort of thing they'd say, 'Oh! It's the 'old boy' again! The 'old boy' wants to learn to drive those horses!

The chaps used to swear then as much as they do now. Oh just as much! But conditions made you swear, like with the trace horses, you only had a rope on one side of the horse! There was nothin' on the right hand side! Just this one plough line to the lead horse on the left!

You controlled the horses with your voice. If you wanted them to go right handed you just shouted 'Wugged!' That was when you wanted them to go 'Frammed'. If you wanted them to turn left it was 'Come here!' Or if you wanted them to come right round 'Come round!' That was to the left which we called 'Tohard'. Actually it should be 'toward' but in Wiltshire - 'tohard'. Now if you wanted to go right round to the right instead of 'Wugged!' it was 'Wa-hoot!'. When chaps were ploughin' it sort of became a regular thing to do to talk to them, the horse would be in the furrow not varying much an inch but you'd be talkin' to the horses all the time. 'Come ere - come here! Wugged, wugged!' All the time! Of course if was as much to amuse himself as to instruct the horse. It was amazing how the horses that had been properly trained could do that. We carted corn sometimes without touching the horse. We'd take the corn to the stack an' then drive back up to the field just shoutin'! No reins at all!

They were all trained on the job. At Knighton they always had six or seven colts a year an' they'd put each one between two trained horses. We usually ploughed with three horses an' the colt was tied back in the middle, so that he had to do what the others did. He couldn't get away, you see! You had plough lines to the two an' the colt just had to go where they went! The colt was tied mouth to mouth on the bits an' also from the head to the collars of the two each side, crossed over, like that.

When you were harrowin' you'd have two or three, or even four horses an' they had head sticks on from one bit to the other. You just put your reins on the nearside horse an' when they were workin' so you only drove the nearside horse but you had to remember that were turning'. If you didn't turn soon enough the outside horse would be up in the hedge, upside down an' all sorts of things! But eventually you learnt an' it all came as a matter of course. After a few times you did it automatically.

In the mornin's we had to get there at half past six. The carter would have been up at four o'clock an' fed the horses, an' we would then clean the horses, harness them an' get them out by half past seven. There was an hour for dinner in the field then you left the field at half past three. We went home at five o'clock. We'd always take nosebags out with the horses, one to each horse, hung on the hames. We always rode 'side saddle'. You put your foot in the traces to hook yourself up, then out we all went, the carter in front then the second in command and so on down to the old boy at the back, he was the last one. The carter at Knighton was a wonderful old boy really, although we used to play him up no end. I think that there was three of us boys there, an' we'd play all the tricks on any of them. The carter was gettin' older an' he couldn't get up on this big horse. A huge horse called 'Blossom'. Got a back like an armchair. He couldn't get up like we could, being young, an' he always used to say, 'Give us a leg up boy'. An' one of the boys said, 'I've got fed up leggin' him up', he said, 'If he asks me tomorrow mornin' I'll leg him up!' An' he did! He legged him up an' the old carter went straight over the top an' slid down the other side! You ought to have heard the old man talk! It was a silly thing to do really.

The old carter lived in one of the cottages at the T junction, at the Ramsbury turn. The farm blacksmith lived in the other. Most farms of that size had their own blacksmith an' farrier. He was in charge of all the tackle. If you wanted plough shares or plough lines, you had to go to him. You never asked the boss.

Mr Gore, the boss at Knighton, used to come down at seven o'clock in the mornin', but he never came in the stable. He always leaned over the bottom stable door an' the carter leant on the other side, talkin'. He would say what he wanted done, an' us boys would be round the corner, listenin'! Tryin' to sort out which job we were goin' to have. He didn't always want us to go ploughin'. Some of us would go 'arrowin' an odd field. One of you cartin' stuff for the sheep. Whatever it was, we'd be round the corner sortin' it out! But when it boiled down to it, you did what the carter said. That's what you did! His word was law! He told you which horses to have. He'd name them. He'd say, 'You have so and so' to one, an' to the other, 'An' you have Captain, Charger an' Boxer'. I suppose it was a good idea because you got used to all of them. There was eight horses in one stable, all in a line, no partitions or stalls. They stood side by side, an' the chaff coop an' the corn bin was in the middle. The buildin' continued the other side with the rest of the horses. Seventeen all together. There was a hayloft over so that the hay could be put down into the racks. The horses were always turned out at night, into the yard. There was a horse yard in front of the stable. The horses were only tied up to be fed, an' cleaned an' harnessed. When the carter started at four in the mornin' he'd let the horses into the stables an' they'd all go to their own places an' stand to be tied up to be fed. Sometimes a colt might go in the wrong place but the old horses would put him right, an' make him go where he was supposed to go.

When we got in at night there was unharnessin' an' cleanin'. We were often tired after a hard day's ploughin' an' so, when the carter used to say, 'Put the brush over these horses boy,' Bert Giddings would get to the top of the stable an' when the carter wasn't lookin' he'd throw the brush right down over the top of the horses to me at the bottom! An' I'd throw it back to him underneath! Then the old feller would come in an' say, 'Have you put the dandy brush over these horses?'

'Oh yeh!' we'd say, 'We've been over them an' under them!' But of course sometimes we hadn't touched them! We were too worn out! Perhaps sometimes we used to clean the back parts where he could see.

Horses weren't clipped out at all. They'd just be left ordinary. But they never got colds although they'd often be sweatin' when they came in from the fields. Of course they'd stand in the stable from four until half five before bein' turned out into the yard so by that time they had stopped sweatin'.

That was how it was at Thomas Gore's farm at Knighton. But Gores had another farm at Oakhill, Froxfield, an' another one at Hungerford Newtown. Sometimes one of us boys would be sent to Hungerford Newtown to get a load of oats for the horses. You seldom did any other work over at that farm, but we did at Oakhill Farm. They kept no horses at all there. They'd just got this arable land an' when it was ploughin' time all of the horses an' ploughs were taken over there from Knighton. The ploughs were loaded onto wagons, taken to Oakhill an' all the ploughin' done in one go. This would take days an' Gore provided us with bicycles to ride home on at night after the horses had been turned out. You see, they had stables over there ... an' in the mornin' we'd ride back to Oakhill on the bicycles. We had to be there by seven. One chap though, used to walk from Ramsbury! He used to go up the hill to Froxfield. There used to be a footpath nearly all the way. He would always get there before us!

They didn't grow any hay at Oakhill, just corn. But harvestin' was arranged just the same as the ploughin'. Everyone would go over there with the tackle an' it was all done at once. The stacks were made on hard standin' where the threshin' tackle could get to in the winter.

It was different at Knighton where all the corn was taken back to the farm. Much easier! The straw stacks had to be in the right places where it could be used for the horses and other stock. It was all long straw then, there were no balers an' corn was bagged into West of England sacks. These were hired from the sack merchant. They held four bushels; two an' a quarter hundredweight for wheat, two hundredweight for barley, an' two an' a half hundredweight for beans. They took some humpin' about! Although we never grew any beans at Knighton. When I was seventeen I was carryin' these sacks up the granary steps an' tippin' them over into the bin. No wonder I was tired at nights! You'd move each bag two or three times. You loaded them up at the thresher, jumped up on the wagon an' moved them back, an' then taken then back to the farm an' carried them up these steps - at night, you'd be knackered!

As recent as the Second World War I've moved twenty tons twice a day, comin' off the thresher, loadin' them up, takin' the wagon into the barn, pickin' up the sacks an' runnin' up a board an' tippin' them in a bin.

Threshin' was always a dirty, itchin' job! The earlier in the season you could do it, the better. When you had to leave it to March it was terrible, especially if there was thistles in it! In those days there was no sprays to kill thistles, well, there was brown oil of vitriol, which some folks used to spray from a horse drawn sprayer which had a big wooden barrel. When there were thistles, not only was threshin' bad but shockin' up was painful. They'd stick into your legs through your trousers an' all your forearms would be sore. 'An if it was wet, it was really terrible!

People today have no idea what we had to put up with!

Don't you remember that particularly bad harvest you had at Littlecote Park Farm when the corn in the Barnfield, which was about a hundred acres, went down! The straw was lyin' in all directions! They got out the hooks and scythes and some of the sheaves they made were ten foot long!

That was hard work, but then so was most farm work, an' we didn't get paid much! I think I got seven bob at Knighton. When I was workin' for Days at Whittonditch I cut an acre of vetches with a hook on my own! But he never worried you, he never came an' said, 'It's about time you got a move on!' he just let me go on in me own sweet way. He was a nice man. The carter did all the binderin' at Knighton. But if they had two binders, the under-carter had the other binder. Gores had two or three binders but most places only had one. There was an art in that job, knowin' how to thread the needle, an' how the string went, you had to get it exactly right! It's like a sewin' machine. If you didn't get it right, it wouldn't tie. It would get all knotted up an' if you had to cut the twine off the knotters you had to be careful not to let your knife mark the knotter bills 'cause then the twine would hang up worse! On most binders you had three canvasses conveying the corn and you had to know which one was which otherwise it wouldn't work. They were made with wooden slats rivetted across every so often an' they were strapped round the rollers with leather straps an' buckles. The binder in those days seemed to be quite a complicated piece of machinery, an' to us it was, but it led the way to more modern machinery. I mean modern balers use virtually the same knotter mechanism, some of the simple machines have yet to be bettered. Even in the 1940s I drilled all the mangolds an' all the kale with one of those little Planet drills. It was a push one. At first I had an outrigger with a markin' peg to mark out the next drill but that was added work. So what I did was, I had an old fashioned horse hoe that you could open or shut an' you'd got five or six tines on it. Well, I fixed a long piece of wood across the back an' then bolted four pieces of angle iron to it spaced out so that they would scratch the ground an' mark out the row. A girl led the horse an' of course I marked out three more rows with every bout, because the fourth tine was kept on the last mark.

Another problem we used to solve in an old fashioned way was when the leather-jackets kept eatin' the kale when it was just comin' through the ground. You had to get a pound or two of Paris Green an' you mixed it with about a 'hundredweight of bran an' then put a little handful every yard or so up the row. The first two or three rows were quite O.K. but there were a lot of rows in the field, an' very soon your back ached an' your legs ached an' you got fed up with walkin'. An' all the time I'm thinkin' about how I can make it easier. So, instead of bendin' down I tried droppin' a handful of bran down the side of me leg! But the wind blew the bran away! So when I went home to dinner I got a flexible spout from the corn drill an' I tried that down the side of me leg an' made a funnel out of a bit of roofin' felt, an' fixed that to the top. Then, as the leg went forward, I dropped this handful of bran in the funnel, an' where me foot stopped, it left the bran in a perfect pyramid! An' that simple idea turned a back-breakin' job into an everyday walk!

Then there was the basic slag. We used to put the slag on the kale to kill the flea beetle, or at least, keep it off. Well, slag is very heavy stuff an' we used to put it in a sandbag an' you went down the field shakin' it so that the dust fell down on the row. Well, that was a monotonous job. So I put the buck-rake on the tractor an' got the cowman an' four others to sit across the back. I put the tractor into top gear an' the job was soon done. I was always figurin' ways to make work easier. If you did that, then you could get more work done without too much hassle.

The boss once told Mary that he wouldn't mind bein' stranded on a desert island with me 'cause he reckoned what whatever the problem was I'd find some way of gettin' over it!

I suppose I inherited a lot of that outlook from my father. Although he was very good with anything metal, he wasn't such a good gardener. He used to grow stuff, but not as good as Sid or me. But he was wonderful with iron! They had no electric welders in those days, so if Dad wanted to weld two pieces of metal together he'd put them into the fire until they was the right heat, an' then he'd whip them out on to the anvil an' give it one bang to weld it an' then shape it up. All the harrow tines used to wear out an' sometimes they'd come in when they was only three inches long. He'd take all the worn tines out, well they were only held in by a bit of metal or an horse nail - they weren't bolted, they were square at the top an' wedged into the hole with an "L"-shaped" key. I think that they were peculiar to Wiltshire. Well when the worn tines were taken out they were lengthened by weldin' another piece of iron onto them. He'd put the worn tine an' another bit of metal in the fire an' flatten both ends out, an' take two tongs an' bring both pieces on to the anvil an' with just that one bang they were welded. Of course, he had to reheat them to finish them off. That's how the tyres on the waggons were welded. Franklins, down Oxford Street, did the woodwork. They were the wheelwrights, an' when the wheels were ready to be bonded one of their sons used to push these wheels down to the blacksmith's at the bottom of Blind Lane.

When he had about eight or ten he'd put all the bonds on. They had to be measured beforehand with a little wheel called a 'traveller'. They'd put a chalk mark on both the disc an' the wheel an' then run the traveller round the wheel countin' the revolutions an' when the traveller came back to the chalk mark on the wheel they marked the traveller again. That way the blacksmith knew exactly how much iron was needed to make the band. The weldin' they called 'shuttin''. They always said 'Cut an' Shut!' It was never called weldin'!

As I said, Franklins were wheelwrights, coachbuilders and undertakers. The Franklins who ran *The Bell* an' the butchers were a different family. Freddy, the grandson of the old man, was still there when I last heard, still runnin' the business. His father was Joshua Franklin an' he had a brother named Arthur Franklin who used to keep a cow in a little field. When Arthur was ill I used to get up early an' milk this cow before I went to work, I'd milk it again when I came home at night. That was when I was with Willie Hobbs. I went to Willie Hobbs after I left Gores at Knighton. When I told Gore I was leavin' he was quite concerned about it. He didn't want me to leave! 'What was wrong with the place? What didn't I like about it?' I think that the carter had told him that as I was the youngest boy I had to have the worst bike when they went to Oakhill, an' I didn't like it! You see, like the best horses, it all went in order. The oldest had the best bikes, down to the youngest, an' that was me! So I had to have the old one!

But my leavin' Gores had nothin' at all to do with that! It was just that instead of havin' to walk a mile every mornin' I'd just got two minutes down the street! Actually, I wished I'd never left! I was happier workin' with several people than I was with just one. Willie Hobbs only had a small farm, so there was just two of us there, the carter and me. Of course, we got extra people when we were harvestin' an' haymakin'. The farm buildin's were down Oxford Street next to Charlie Sparrow's on the right, an' the land was up the back. Some of it up Crowood Lane.

One of the jobs I did there that the carter wouldn't do happened like this.

One summer, one of the horses put his head round to bite at a fly, an' he caught his eyebrow on the hook where the traces used to go on, an' he tore his eyebrow right along. Now Willie Hobbs would never have a vet! He never had a vet all the time I was there! So when I came home at night Willie Hobbs said to Jim Gray, who was the carter, 'Look at what old Prince has done! You'll have to sew that up!' An' Jim said, 'I can't do it!' So Willie Hobbs said, 'Well, Gordon'll have to do it then.' So I said, 'Why must I do it? He's the carter!'

So Willie Hobbs said, 'Go round to the shoemaker's shop an' get some wax-ends' (that's the piece of thread with wax on it that you use to sew your shoes) an' get a needle. You'll find one there with a bit of a crook in it.'

So I got this needle an' thread an' Willie said, 'Thread it! an' we'll hold the horse while you do the sewin'.'

So they get this twitch on the horses's nose an' they stood me on this box an' do you know the job I had to get that needle through that horse's skin? It was so hard! Well, I managed to sew the gap up with about four stitches an' it healed with no trouble at all. After a couple or three months, you'd never had known it'd been done! I'd have been about eighteen then.

I only stayed with Willie Hobbs two or three years. He was a lay preacher an' on several Sundays of the year he would go to other parishes to preach. He had a couple of cows an' he looked after those all the week himself. But when he was preachin', I used to have to milk the cows. Before he went off, Willie Hobbs used to say, 'Make sure you clean the stable out!' Well after I'd been doin' this for several Sundays, I saw what he was doin' from about Thursday was chuckin' all the manure in a heap, just inside the shed! He was chuckin' it up in a corner! So when I came on a Sunday I had to clean out the muck of three or four days! So I said to him about it an' he said, 'Oh he hadn't done that!' However, for the Sunday work he paid me somethin' like a shillin', but not until the end of the year when he paid me so many shillin's for what I'd done for the whole year, an' when I told him I was goin' to leave to go up to Kent, he didn't like it, because he had to get somebody else. I suppose somebody who was as much of a big fool as what I'd been!

When he finally paid me my wages, I think it was about twenty-seven an' six, I said, 'What about my Sunday money then?' Because I was relyin' on that little bit. I didn't have any money much, an' I needed it to pay my train fare. I said, 'What about the money for lookin' after the cows?' He said, 'Oh, I've only been away about three Sundays!' I said, 'That's neither here nor there. Your stipulation when I came was that you'd pay me so much per year, it doesn't matter how many Sundays you say you've been out!' Well, he eventually paid me but he didn't like it.

After I left an' went up to Kent, I went home for a holiday, an' Willie Hobbs was soon round to me to come an' stack for him. That's where I learnt stackin', an' that was only because nobody else would do it. At Gores I hadn't had a chance to do any stackin' because we did nothin' else but horses. Nothing else!

As I said at Knighton Farm we worked six days a week but finished at four o'clock. But I remember one Saturday when it was the football match between Ramsbury an' Aldbourne. We asked if we could stop work at two o'clock! He said, 'The next thing you'll be wantin' will be a holiday!'

That would be about the time the farmers screwed the wages down. If you didn't accept less from the man you were workin' for, there was always someone who would offer to work for less still! Just so as to get a job!

Farmers always said they couldn't pay, but very few knew whether they could pay or not, because not many kept accounts. Most deals were cash, an' that's how it went.

Then I worked one time for Charlie Day at Whittonditch. That was when I worked with "Monster". Charlie Day had three sons, Charlie, Norman an' Roland. They were really political! They often talked about Foot, that'd be Michael Foot's father. In those days the root crops were rarely clean. Of course, that's why they were grown! To clean the land with hoes at least once in the rotation. You could hardly see the rows for fat hen an' twitch an' nearly every weed under the sun. They weren't horse-hoed before, they were just a mass of weeds. We hoed as a gang, an' as I was only a boy I was put between the men. If you went in front, you didn't go fast enough, an' if you were at the back, you couldn't keep up! So they put me in the middle.

I was always next to a man called Tom Dixon, whose family lived at Crowood, at *The Fox an' Hounds*. They were a large family an' all very big men. Tom was about six feet an' he had a great bull neck. It all came up from his shoulders to his chin. But he was very good to me. He was as good as a second father, He used to bring me an apple or a cake each day. Anyway, when we were hoein' I used to get next to him an' every so often he'd hoe a bit in my row, so that I could catch up.

We always seemed to be hoein' mangolds from eight o'clock until four, possibly later. After I left there I was talkin' to "Monster" an' he said, 'Old Charlie Day reckoned that you were one of the best hoers that he'd ever had!' I said, 'Well, why didn't he tell me that when I was there?' You see that would have made a lot of difference, wouldn't it? Apparently he reckoned that I hoed everythin' twice! We always had long-handled hoes. We stood upright, but it still used to make your back ache! Even today, after seventy years I always follow the same procedure that Tom Dixon learnt me all those years ago, o'course now it's only carrots an' parsnips in the garden. But Tom used to say, 'Always keep your eye ahead boy for the single one an' then you don't have to do any thinnin's', an' if you do that, you can hoe accordin'. An' that's a good policy, not only do you avoid disturbin' the single plants, but you don't have to bend down so often to single the bunches! It's not so much whether you can stand up an' hoe, it's this up an' down business that makes your back ache so bad! My back used to ache terrible! Sometimes I could hardly walk home, yet' after you'd been home for a while an' you'd had your tea, you'd be out, an' up the lane, playin'!

In those days, farmers kept a lot of their own seed corn, an' cleaned an' dressed it themselves. They'd mix it up with such seed dressin' as there was, on the barn floor, with a shovel. They would seldom buy any in unless theirs got too bad. I used to put the corn in with an old Suffolk steerage drill. That was, one bloke walkin' behind to see that the corn went down the drill, one bloke steerin' it, an' me with four horses, two in front an' two behind. At Witcha Farm, there was quite a few banks there an' they wanted four horses to pull it up there really. These Suffolk drills were quite big, an' you still had just this one rope to the left-hand front horse, you had no rein to pull them to the right! That was done by shoutin'.

If you was an inch out in the rows folks 'ud want to know if you'd gone on your holidays! They always used to say that you had to make the horses go the same pace up hill an' down! Now how could a boy of thirteen drive four horses up hill an' down? The rope was tied from the trace horse to the nearside one on the thill. That was the one at the back. They were tied across from bit to bit. If one did more work than the other, you tied them back accordin'.

Now, about these Wiltshire terms.

The horse that was in the shafts was in the 'thills', an' the ridge chain that supported the shafts on the pad was the 'rudgesty'. Then the short traces in the cart were 'tugs' an' most of the other things like breechin' was the same as elsewhere.

Well, for now, that's about all I can call to mind about life in Ramsbury. I expect that I'll think of a bit more later on, we'll have to see!"

GORDON

A NEW LIFE IN KENT

In 1927, Gordon left Ramsbury to take a job as a gardener with Mr & Mrs Mantle at Hitherfield, Knockholt in Kent.

"When I went to Knockholt first, I went in the gardens. They had a chauffeur, an' I lived with him an' his wife. There was a room for the married couple an' a bed sittin' room for me in this little bungalow. The chauffeur's wife looked after me.

They had a Rover car, a 14 horse-power; 1921 it was made, a tourer with an open top. An' with two windscreens. One at the front an' one to fix in front of the back seats. The windscreen frames were all made of brass; beautifully made! In the summer the top would be down an' you could open the front windscreen a little bit at the bottom to let the cool air rush through. The hand-brake was outside the car an' only worked on the back two wheels, but I think that the foot-brake worked on the transmission. Oil used to drop on the transmission so half the time the foot-brake was no good at all! It was a great long hand-brake, I suppose about two-foot six long an' if you pulled this on really hard the whole back used to jump up an' down!

One of the highlights of my life was when the chauffeur left. Mr Mantle said, 'Do you know C... was leavin?'. I said 'Yes' an' so he said, 'Would you like to learn to drive the car?'

Of course, to a country-bloke like me who'd only worked with horses, learnin' to drive a car was somethin'!

Well, I agreed, an' Mr Mantle said that Mr Roland, his son, would learn me to drive. We went out the next Saturday afternoon to Rushmoor Hill. We got to the top an' he said, 'Now you get in the drivin' seat an' steer. So we went down the hill with no engine runnin', just coastin' down. We coasted down to the end at Pratt's Bottom, turned round, an' he drove it back up. Then we went down again.

We did that about a half a dozen times. Then he said, 'Now you drive it back up!' He told me which was the gears an' within about three weeks I was takin' the Old Man to the station. On cold mornin's, the oil was so thick that to fill up the gearbox you had to warm the oil first to get it to flow through the 'ole! I used to think that there was something wrong with the gears sometimes when I couldn't get it in gear, it was a terrible job.

Anyway, I drove it for quite a long time an' I can never remember havin' a new silencer or battery, or anthing new on it! It seemed to go on an' on for ever! It was very well built. The wings were so thick that you could kick them an' never make a dent in them!

One mornin' I was down at Fox's Garage at Badger's Mount gettin' some petrol an' the chap said to me, 'When you gonna get a new car?' An' I said, 'Not til I smash this one up I suppose!' An' then, lo an' behold, on the way home I met a lorry on the corner, an' I had to run right up the bank! But he didn't! An' he took me wing off! Well, next door to took it off. An' then, in about a couple of months I got a new one!

The car was a Morris. The company had brought two cars out an' they called them 'fabric' saloons, an' I've never ever seen any since. They were a wooden framework with fabric over them like an aeroplane. Ours was a Morris Oxford an' a very small one, perhaps the forerunner of the Morris Minor. That would be about 1930, They never caught on, but they were quiet to drive; they were saloons.

Once I went with them to Lincoln, an' comin' back down the Great North Road, I had a big-end go! It was the other side of Barnet, so we had to come home by train an' taxis. I had to go back to Barnet the followin' week to pick the car up.

At that time, I was chauffeur-gardener. I took the Old Man to the station every mornin' at half-past seven, an' every night he came home on the six-eight train. He was a collar manufacturer. They made ladies' collars an' cuffs. But during the war they made stuff for the forces. He used all the off-cuts from the khaki shirts an' made them into shirts for the boys at Dr. Barnado's. The factory got bombed two or three times with fire-bombs!

He was always very proud of the fact that he came to London with only five pounds in his pocket. He came from the Isle of Sheppey. At first he worked in a shop on the Isle of Sheppey. Then he came to London an' worked for a firm called Stollery an' Fifield an' it was they who made women's collars an' cuffs an' things. I think he said that he'd been there about two or three years an' thought that he wasn't gettin' on fast enough an' he decided to get another job. But they said, 'Would he stay?'. They offered him more money. An' he said, 'No!. The only reason I'll stay on is if you make me a partner in the firm'. An' that's what they did! Eventually he owned the firm on his own!

At one time my brother, Sid, worked at Knockholt. I heard a job was goin' an' I fetched Sid up from Wiltshire. They wanted a gardener. Mr P... was the head gardener, but Sid came out of the gardens at Ramsbury Manor an' he knew much more than P...! He left the Manor 'cause they were very poorly paid. I think it would have been in Sir Francis Burdett's time. Most of these big places paid less if they could, you really had to pay for the privilege of workin' for them!

This feller P... would sell anything he could get hold of at *The Oak*. If his boss ordered a lot of daffodil bulbs his garden would only get half an' the rest were sold up at *The Oak*! That sort of thing!

At that time my brother Sid wasn't married but he'd been goin' out with Ciss Chandler, the gamekeeper's daughter from Park, an' eventually she came up as well. She'd been trained as a tailor an' dressmaker in Ramsbury, an' she got a job as a seamstress at Croydon which wasn't too far from Knockholt. An' Gladys, my sister, also worked at Knockholt. I can't remember how long she stayed, but she was there quite a while.

Sid used to ride the old 1921 Sunbeam motorbike I had when he went to Croydon. He got pulled up once for makin' too much noise! He said he had to pay ten bob! It grieved him! He said that it was my bike an' yet he had to pay ten bob! That was my first bike. It was a beautiful bike. The chains ran in an oil-bath. There was no kick-start, you just had to push it to start. It had acetylene lightin' an' you had a little pump on the side of the petrol tank for the oil. As long as that kept drippin' you knew you were alright. You had to pump it two or three times, it had a little tube on, an' you could see it drippin', just a drop, every so often. Three an' a half horse-power it was! I drudged a field with it once! I made a drudge out of wire-nettin' an' put it on the back an' drudged the field with it. Drudged? Chain harrowed in Wiltshire, it's drudged in Kent. I had a lump of wood to keep it taut, that was to spread the cow-dung! At one time, in Wiltshire, they used to make harrows out of holly bushes an' thorns. If they were just laid out nicely with a couple of logs across to keep down, they'd last a surprisin' long time!

I did most of Mrs Mantle's shoppin' an' errands in the village as I took him to an' fro from the station. Every night I used to have to go into the kitchen an' she'd give me a list of things she'd want at the Post Office or the shop, an' she'd give me the money.

Else I would pay out of me own money, an' then I'd get the money off of her at the end of the week. I used to get the bills for the petrol an' then she'd settle. If she owed you a ha'penny she would pay, an' if I owed her a ha'penny she would tell me! Everything was always settled! She was very careful. Even the butter paper was always scraped clean! Perfectly!

What I missed when I first went to Knockholt was food. At home, in Ramsbury, if the food was there, we ate until we were full up! But the Mantles ate very little! When I first went to Knockholt, if the chauffeur's wife was away, Mrs Mantle used to look after me. I used to go over there for meals, an' it wasn't enough to feed a sparrow with! But they weren't workin' you see! They didn't need it! But I was always hungry! I mean a couple of thin little bits of bread an' butter for a bloke who was diggin' all day! That was no good was it? I expect that's how they became rich!

They was Methodists. Sometimes I used to have an argument with Mr Mantle about gamblin'. I said to him, 'Well, you buy things on the stock exchange an' hope to make a bit of money! Well gamblin's just the same really', 'cause he couldn't really answer that could he?

But he was always very fair. Of course, nobody got very much in wages. When I went to work there I got thirty-eight shillings a week an' that was quite a rise from Ramsbury where it was twenty-seven an' six!

Then I had to pay the chauffeur's wife for my keep, but what Mr Mantle suggested me payin', she said, wasn't enough! So he had to make up my wages two or three shillings. The chauffeur's wife wasn't a very good housewife, but he was a nice chap. She came from Frinton-on-Sea an' had been a typist, or something like that. They left when she was expectin'. She didn't want to have her baby in Knockholt, so she returned to her mother at Frinton.

SETTLED IN

I suppose that Mr Mantle was as good as anybody else, but I would never creep to him. The others seemed to be always on the fiddle. Like the last cowman who used to keep a few chicken. He used to say, 'Roly, can I have a bag of hay to put in my rabbits?' Of course Roly said, 'Yes' but when the cowman went home, in the bottom of the bag he'd got wheat! He thought I was stupid. But I wasn't as daft as that! There's a difference between hay an' corn in a bag. But in spite of the fiddles the chaps weren't a bad lot really.

I remember once that I'd arranged to go to Wembley to see the final of the dirt-track racin'. I'd told Roly long before that I was goin' an' he'd agreed. Well, it came one day when we were cartin' wheat. I said, 'Don't forget, Roly, I'm goin' off this afternoon.' An' he said, 'You can't go!' an' I said, 'Why not?' 'Well,' he said, 'We got nobody to make the stack'. So I said, 'There's four or five others, let one of them make it!'

An' so I went!

The next mornin' there was a bit of a row but Mr Mantle said that if I'd made previous arrangements to have the afternoon off then I was entitled to go. But the point was that none of the others would make the stack an' poor old Roly had to try an' do it himself! He came to me an' said that the stack would have to be remade an' would I do it! So we unloaded the stack on to the ground an' on to the wagons an' I built it up again.

Mrs Mantle would have everything done just so. She wouldn't throw anything away unnecessarily. She used to tell me how many runner beans to pick an' the rest just went to waste. Knowin' how she was, I suppose I used to grow too many. The same as broad beans. She used to want me to pick them when they were too small! I didn't like that but it was up to her! It was their beans after all! But they didn't each much. Do you know, they once served me up junket! Well I mean, that wasn't any good to me! A spoonful of junket. An' me diggin' out there all day on that old stony ground!

When I became chauffeur I used to have to wear a uniform. Peaked cap, thick cloth jacket an' breeches, leggin's an' boots. After a bit he changed the uniform from breeches to trousers. In the summer I had a white linen coat which had been C...'s, the chauffeur before me, an' there was a cream linen cover for the cap. The ugliest outfit you ever saw! Then he bought me an alpaca, a blue one! You could have got ten people inside it! When I used to get out of the car I felt awful. You could have wrapped it round me a couple of times! I always wore stiff white collars an' I often shaved twice a day!

Mr Mantle would ride in the front seat when I took him to the station, but he'd sit in the back when his wife was with him. There was a lot of toffs used to come on the six-eight train. There could be anything from ten to fifteen chauffeurs down there. Everybody used to try an' get away first! Talk about a racetrack! Mr Mantle said, 'Don't you trouble about standin' outside openin' the door, you stay in the drivin' seat with the car in gear!' He used to come out of the station an' jump in the car, an' if we got in front, nobody'd pass us! What's more if we got in front we wouldn't let anybody else come by!

When it was foggy it was a different thing. We used to have some terrible fogs, often you couldn't see your hand in front of your face! Of course, when it was foggy, everyone used to wait for somebody else to move off first, so that you could follow them!

Sometimes Mr Mantle would go on as if he owned the place! An' me bein' a country bloke, it used to rile me no end! I mean there were people comin' off the train who lived close to the station an' who used to walk. They'd come out of the station walk a little way up the path an' then cross over the road. Some nights these two or three chaps would walk across the road in front of us an' I would have to wait! One night when this 'appened, Mr Mantle said, 'Pull up at the side of those people there, Hiscock.' So I pulled up at the side of them an' he wound down the window an' said, 'Look, it would be quite a good idea if you walked up the path the whole way, an' let the cars get out!' So you can guess what they told him he could do with his car! Then when we got to the top, instead of turnin' left towards home he said, 'Turn right!', an' he made me pull up alongside the same chaps again. He wound down the window an' he said, 'Would you like a lift?' Well, I admired his sauce, but you can imagine what they told him he could do with his lift as well!

When we went over to mains electricity, Mr Mantle sold this electric light engine an' there was a diddykai or someone came up the drive an' asked if we had got an electric light plant. I told him we had, an' as Mr Mantle was in the garden, he went up to him an' said, 'Will you sell me your electrifc light plant mister?' Mr Mantle said 'Yes', so the chap said, 'Well how much do you want for it?' 'Ten pounds' said Mr Mantle. The man was taken aback. 'Oh, I couldn't give you that' he said, 'I'll give you eight'. 'No,' said Mr Mantle, 'Ten pounds'. Well the man started umin' an' ahin' an' Mr Mantle said, 'Now look here, if you offered me nine pounds nineteen shillings and elevenpence three farthings I wouldn't take it. It's ten pounds or get out of my drive and back on the road!'

Mr Mantle was that sort of man. His word was his bond. If he said he wanted ten pounds, then he wanted ten pounds. He was a bit of a stickler on some things.

He always called me 'Hiscock' never 'Mr Hiscock!' or for that matter 'Gordon'. But like many others with domestic servants, the men were always called by their surnames an' the women an' girls by their christian names. That'd be called sexual harrassment now! Although they possibly only want to impose their social superiority by usin' surnames, it used to make me cross. He called me 'Hiscock' an' all his family called me 'Hiscock' as well, but I could put up with that, but when his chauffeur left an' an old lady came in to look after me, she called me 'Hiscock' too! The people who worked in his factory an' some of the people I took messages to, they called me 'Hiscock' an' that used to get me down. Even when I was at the farm, people might come to the door an' ask if 'Hiscock' was about. Some of them didn't even have money! But of course then money is nothin'! It's the principle of it. Even the two girls who worked for him in the city an' who came to live in the cottage after we moved to the farm used to call me 'Hiscock' just the same. In Wiltshire we always called the boss by his christian name. It was never 'mister' to anybody. Bosses an' men were on christian names terms. When I worked for Willie Hobbs in Ramsbury, Jim Gray, the carter, always called him 'Bill', never 'Mister Hobbs'!

The so-called 'upper classes' were pretty arrogant. I mean if some of them had a domestic workin' for them an' they didn't like her name, they'd change it! Take Mrs Buxty. Her name was 'Violet' but they didn't like it so they called her 'Lily'! That was all wrong. An' Iris Lovelace they used to call 'Ethel'!

But it's this misuse of surnames that gets me. I mean, when the upper classes call you by your surname it's to put you down an' keep you in your place, but when the underlings use it they're only doin' it to lift themselves up!

Yet although I always say that they treated me fairly, that isn't to say that it was in any way generous. For instance, when we went to the farm he never let us have any milk. An' with our big family! Not a drain of milk! But in other ways he was quite good. He paid our electric bill. But that was only because of a mistake really. When we went to the farm, instead of the Board sendin' the bill to us, they sent it to him. He thought that we'd told them to send it to him. So he paid it! He told me about it afterwards, but I told him that we didn't know anything about it! We'd never had a bill! So he continued to pay it but said, 'Don't tell the others!'

Then, when the kitchen garden became vacant round at his house, he said, 'Would you like to have the garden and plant it up?'. An' so I said, 'Well, I might just as well!'. So I borrowed a Trusty tractor from Jack Dewberry, I ploughed it up, cultivated it an' put this an' that in an' got it beautiful! Then one mornin' Roly said, 'Father wants to see you. Will you go round to the house and have a word with him?'

So I went round an' he said to me, 'When I woke up this morning I saw a beautiful sight. All those heifers from the field next door were lying in your garden amongst what was left of your cabbages! Somebody had forgot to shut the wicket gate!'. So what he did was to pay me so much in compensation. An' that was very fair, I thought!

But to get back to the chauffeurin'. I used to have to open the car door for him, although it would sometimes depend on the occasion. If I picked them both up from the station I would stand by the car with the door open an' with the rug over my arm. When they sat down, I draped the rug across their knees. It was sort of a carry-on from horse-drawn days!

The chauffeurs at Knockholt Station all did the same. We must have had a lot in common. If it was a foggy night an' the train was late we all used to congregate in the porter's room an' sit there yarnin'. When the train came in we'd go outside an' say 'Who's goin' to go first?'.

If it was a foggy night and Mr Roland was on the train I used to get him to drive an' I used to sit in the passenger seat, wind the window right down, lean out an' tell him where he was on the road! There was Bowen's timber yards just this side of Knockholt Station an' they had these great huge trees stacked at the side of the road, well just the footpath away. Then I saw one of these trees right in front an' I shouted 'Stop!'. He stopped dead about a foot away! Well we backed off an' it was alright! I don't know why the fogs were so bad in those days, I suppose it was all the coal that was being burnt, you never get the fogs now.

Although I suppose that there's always worse fogs at Pratt's Bottom by Knockholt Station. Once I had to meet Mr Mantle's nieces on a Saturday afternoon an' the fog was so bad that he said, 'When you go down to pick them up, you'd better take Belcher (that was the chap that worked with me) 'cause they say it's so bad down there'. I went an' when we were comin' from the station it was so bad that I couldn't see. So I said 'You walk in front Harry!' An' do you know, even with him walkin' in front we missed the turnin'!

Sometimes the mist used to clear as you went up the hill to Knockholt, but not always. There's been many a time when I've run off the road in the fog! Of course, lights weren't so good then an' puttin' yeller over the glass didn't seem to make much difference either! Nine times out of ten it was drivin' by guesswork an' the grace of God, that's all! But apart from that I liked drivin'! But when I gave up drivin' an' returned to farmin' it was like goin' back to my youth. Especially when we got horses! Those Suffolk Punches were beautiful! Then, of course, there was more acres. When I was gardenin' we only had seven acres so I didn't have much chance to do a bit of shootin'. But I was always lookin' for rabbits. I saw one sittin' in a tuft of grass. I scratted about for a couple of stones, missed with the first but bowled him clean over with the second! Clean as a whistle! Mind you, I've shot one or two runnin' away, with a rifle. That takes some doin! I had a bolt action Winchester, a beautiful rifle. I've shot many a rabbit sittin' at a hundred yards, but runnin' away, well two or three I suppose, not more, an' I've shot pheasants at night with it too!

Talkin' about rabbits, sometimes on a Sunday mornin' when Ann was born I'd put her in the pram an' walk down Brasted Hill along Sundridge Road an' come back along up Hogtrough Hill or the other way round an' come out by the church. Well, one Sunday I saw a rabbit in a squat, so I parked the pram, got a couple of stones an' bang! Down he comes, off the bank, rolls into the road, so I pulled his neck to make sure he was dead, an' I put him in the well of the pram. You know, it was an old fashioned pram that you could use havin' two kids sittin' either end with their feet in a well. Anyway, I loaded this rabbit an' forgot about it but some way on I thought, 'I bet that thing's full of fleas!'. So I pulled the clothes off Ann and there was fleas everywhere! 'Cause rabbit fleas won't 'urt you, they don't bite humans much! But it took quite a while to make sure they were all gone! If I'd have taken Ann home covered in fleas you can imagine how Mary would have created!

At that time we were livin' in the chauffeur's quarters across the drive from the house. That was until the war started. That was when Mr Mantle asked me to go farmin'.

Anyway he bought this old farm off of old Sammy Constable. It was only a small farm. Several fields. Roly had done a course in farmin' when he was quite young, somewhere in Lincolnshire I think, that was where he met his wife. Well they bought this farm but they didn't know 'ow to 'arness a horse! They'd never had anything to do with cart horses! They didn't have a clue how to pack an' unpack a binder! They had to have someone who knew these things. Mr Mantle knew that I'd been on farms before I came to him so I was the obvious choice.

The farm which adjoined his property was called Haxlett Wood Farm. Old Sammy Constable had sold all the turf off the farm before we had it an' so in the first year it wouldn't grow anything. Not even weeds! It was terrible! Loam on stones! In fact it had once been called 'Stoney Farm!' Sammy had once grown strawberries an' so we decided to do the same. Mr Mantle did have a farmin' policy an' really he farmed well. So we moved into Hazlett Wood Farm. Our nearest neighbour was Mr Ashby at *The Royal Oak* just up the road. We had to have power on the farm so Mr Mantle went to Suffolk an' bought a couple of fine Punches at the breed sale. Lovely horses. One was ninety guineas an' the other ninety-eight. Then he did a silly thing! He went to Sussex an' bought an' old Sussex Wagon. It was very well built but it was heavy an' the front wheels were so big that they couldn't go under the body an' you needed an acre to turn the thing round. It was delivered to Westerham an' I brought it home with these two horses. It was as much as they could do to pull it up the hill ... empty! Eventually when we bought a tractor we had the shafts took off an' a draw-bar put on. But you still needed a big patch to turn on!

Mr Mantle sold the farm in 1954 an' we left. He'd made arrangements for us to live at the Mount in Knockholt. It really belonged to the church but Mr Mantle had seen them about it. We were there until 1957.

It was while we were at Hazlett Wood farm that Dad fell ill. We weren't on the 'phone but the Ramsbury doctor got the police to come round to me with a message tellin' me to ring him. When I spoke to him he told me that Dad wouldn't last more than a couple of days and that it would be alright if I went down to Ramsbury the next day.

When I got there Dad was downstairs in a single bed across the room from my Mother who had been bed-ridden for some years with arthritis.

Dad looked at me an' said, 'I knew you'd come boy' an' he fell asleep.

Jim Strokes, my brother-in-law who lived with them, had been sittin' up with him at nights so I told him that I would sit up that night with Dad. He slept quite peacefully an' as I sat in the chair beside him I suppose I must have dozed off. I don't know what time it was but when I awoke Dad had gone.

POSTSCRIPT BY LEN NOBLE

POSTSCRIPT

Family associations with Ramsbury were not quite to end with Henry's death. Indeed it was in that year that Olive and I decided to move into the parish. We lived there until 1951 and the following account relates how it all happened.

Len Noble

I first met Olive in the early summer of 1940. It was at Knockholt on the North Downs just above the Weald of Kent. Olive was barely eighteen and I was just twenty-one. Olive had come to work in Knockholt in 1939 and I was in the Army and had been posted from the Royal Artillery depot at Blandford to a unit with its headquarters at Sevenoaks. Our job was to man the searchlights in the Biggin Hill Sector which ran from the heavily defended outskirts of London to the sea. Night fighters had yet to be developed and means of detecting aircraft depended on sound locators. German air attacks by day and by night were frequent and being very close to the airfield at Biggin Hill activity was very high. Since we were at action stations most nights, the only 'free-time' I had was during the day. Of course this suited us very well but it did mean that most of our courting was done to a background of the sights and sounds of war! At the time this seemed to be rather commonplace and it is only with hindsight that the dangers that must have been present became apparent.

Olive returned to Ramsbury and in October 1941 we were married at Swindon. Henry and Leonora were brought over to the wedding from Ramsbury and Hilda did the catering. In spite of the difficulties over clothes' rationing, Olive was in white and, of course, I was in uniform. By that time I was stationed at the 5th A.A. Divisional School in Hampshire so I was able to 'stretch' my 24 hour pass a little! Icing the wedding cake proved to be nearly impossible. White icing was out of the question but there were enough sweet coupons from the ration to give it a good coat of chocolate! J.G. Wise of Rodbourne Road, Swindon provided the cake which cost forty-five shillings with a discount of three shillings! That was then more than a week's wages!

The eighteen carat gold wedding ring cost me fifty shillings and the engagement ring with three diamonds had been about six pounds. So, all in all, it came to quite a lot of money!

We went by bus on our honeymoon to Marlborough where we had booked a room at the Merlin Tea Rooms. According to the bill, which is still preserved, the room and breakfast were seventeen shillings a night, with supper for both of us five shillings and sixpence, and lunch the next day was five shillings and tenpence. Light refreshments were added to the bill and they came to one shilling and sixpence. So the cost of our honeymoon was two pounds, six shillings and tenpence!

Nobody knew where we were to spend our honeymoon, that is until I discovered that I had left my razor and toothbrush at Swindon! So we had to ring up and it was sent to us on the next bus!

Olive brought into our marriage two Wiltshire sayings that have stuck with us! The first pretty well sorts out the question of matrimonial possessions.

It goes,

'What's yours in mine, an' whats mine's me own!'

And the second deals equally adequately with the possibility of chauvinistic domination.

'You can push an' you can shuv', but I'm hanged if I'll be druv'.

The last proverb used to be depicted on a postcard on sale in Marlborough as a fat, reluctant pig sitting firmly on its hunkers, refusing to be moved.

The 5th A.A. Divisional School, based at Wolverton House, Basingstoke was engaged in converting searchlight operation from sound location detection to radar, or S.L.C. as it was called. At that time I had a permanent training detachment sited at Roundwood Farm, Micheldever. It was, therefore, very lucky that I was able to fix up accommodation for us both in a farm cottage close to the site. And so our honeymoon was extended! The only problem was that D.D.T had yet to be invented and our blissful nights became rather restless! The bed was hopping! But to newly weds in a war such problems were insignificant!

That arrangement only lasted a few weeks and we set up home with my parents at Harrow Weald. At least Olive did. She was directed into war work and seems to have spent some time soldering electronic connections on some unidentified secret equipment!

The conversion of units to radar was completed to coincide with the peak of night raids by German bombers. I was posted back to the south-east. There was a lot of devastation but with 24 hours off duty at least once a month I was able to see Olive often.

In 1945 our first child, Carolyn, was born. The war in Europe was at an end and the anti aircraft defences of the country were disbanded. I was sent to Larkhill to convert to field guns with the object, no doubt, of being sent to the Far East. However, someone decided that demobilisation would have to start sometime and those who had joined the army before the war were marked down as being unsuitable to be sent anywhere! So I was able to spend the remaining months of my service at Larkhill where quite a number of army horses had hung on. Someone had the quaint idea that Artillery Officers ought to be able to ride a horse and so there were quite a lot of 'chargers' at The School of Artillery and still more, including some dealers' horses, in the lines of the 4th Field Regiment, whose Commanding Officer happened to be first whip with the Royal Artillery Hunt which was kennelled at Bulford.

I was demobbed in 1946 and now had a wife and child to support. Immediately before the war I had worked for the de Haviland Engine Company so I had to take reinstatement. I don't think that they wanted me (or any other returning soldier) and I certainly didn't want them. Having been with horses before the war I had already decided that if I couldn't make a living with horses I would do the next best thing and go farming! But this was easier said than done! Farmers weren't interested. They still had quite a reserve of labour with prisoners of war and refugees.

While we searched for a solution, in 1947, our second child Tony was born at Harrow Weald. So the economics of the situation became much more important!

For Olive, the situation was complicated by her concern for her grandparents who were now both very infirm. We had tried to help Leonora's immobility by buying her a wheelchair but there was nobody capable of pushing it and we were seventy miles away. I think that the only long journey she made in it was one day when we went down to Ramsbury, and pushed her, in the chair, down through the village, along the footpath past Ramsbury Manor, to South Side Cottage at Axford where Sid and Cis lived with their daughters, June and Maddy. Henry had now become so infirm that a second single bed was fixed up in the tiny living room at Mount Pleasant.

Failing to get direct employment on a farm we resolved to seek the help of the Ex-Service training scheme which sought to place demobbed servicemen on farms. We wrote to the Wiltshire War Agricultural Executive Committee and asked them to find me a place as close as possible to Ramsbury.

In April of 1948 Henry died. I still hadn't got a job on a farm and we were still at Harrow. Olive went to the funeral on the train while I stayed at home to look after Carolyn and Tony.

Shortly after we were all required to attend both Salisbury and Trowbridge for interviews to assess our suitability to enter agriculture. Mr Rochford, the Wiltshire Training Officer, had found a 'willing' training employer in the area we had hoped for. This was Tom Bucknell who was a tenant of the Wills at Littlecote Park Farm which was situated across Littlecote Park from Ramsbury. But Tom Bucknell was not going to buy a pig in a poke! He insisted that if I really wanted to work with him then I would have to work for him for a trial period before moving in to one of his cottages. I thought that this was a bit ridiculous at the time but, thinking back, I suppose he did stand to lose his cottage to a desperate family who had failed to find a home. At that time the combined destruction of houses during the war and the lack of any house building programme for several years was making the search for accommodation pretty desperate.

Leaving de Havilands meant giving up a certain five pounds a week and a house with all mod cons for a primitive cottage at the end of a farm track and about three pounds ten shillings a week! But I suppose the factory shut-down in the winter of 1947 just about decided for me where my interests lay!

I had to take the plunge! So I left Olive with the children at Harrow, put my bike on the train and went off to Hungerford. Tom Bucknell had fixed me up with lodgings with a widow woman who lived opposite *The Pelican* at Froxfield on the Bath Road. It was a taste of things to come! The cottage had no plumbing apart from a pump at the kitchen sink and an outside earth closet!

The three weeks trial period passed quickly and we moved into the farm cottage. This was one of a pair of brick and slate houses situated at the end of a muddy farm track. There was no drainage, no electricity and the bucket closet was at the back of the wash house block a few yards from the back door. There was a single brass water tap in the kitchen-cum-dining room and a coal-fired kitchen range. There was also a sitting room with a fireplace and three bedrooms. The view from the cottage to the north was down the valley across Littlecote Park to Eastridge, behind Chilton Foliat. Close by the cottage, to the south, surrounded by tall elm trees was an ancient thatched barn. The cottage itself faced east towards the main farm buildings.

Alexanders, the Hungerford grocers, sent Mr Bull round every week collecting orders for delivery later. Jack Gregory, the baker at Chilton Foliat, called twice a week and before we left, Mr White from Ramsbury started a mobile greengrocer's business. So I suppose that in spite of being isolated we were well provided for.

Doctor Mills at Ramsbury was our doctor and sometimes he would drive down the pot-holed farm road in his new Austin Sheerline limousine. The mail was delivered daily by a postman on a bicycle who rode out from Hungerford to all the outlying places. Although the farm was in Wiltshire, the postal address was 'Hungerford, Berks' because that was the nearest town. In those days, just after the war, not many people had cars and we only had bicycles. With two small children Olive would push them both in a big old-fashioned pram down to Chilton Foliat, leaving the pram at Jack Gregory's and catch the bus or Barnes' carrier to Hungerford or Ramsbury. I suppose it wasn't too bad going down to Chilton but coming back up that long hill by Littlecote with a pram loaded with two children and shopping was a very strenuous exercise.

Sometimes Tom Bucknell would lend us the battered old farm van if we had something urgent but eventually we saved enough money to buy a vehicle. This was a secondhand Austin van. We bought it from Mr Stone at Froxfield. Previously it had been a milk delivery van belonging to Browns the dairymen at Chilton. They had sold it with the front axle broken and Mr Stone had welded it up again! I don't suppose that would have passed an MOT, but in those days such things were yet to be. Anyway, it wasn't too bad, and there was always Fred Skippence at the Froxfield garage to help out.

It's true that the king-pins had more than a bit of wear and that probably caused it to wobble just a bit. Rather than steer, it was best to fix your eye on some distant object along the road and navigate accordingly! It could be quite unnerving! Olive couldn't drive but she did have a go in the thing and actually drove through Ramsbury and up the hill by the Manor. But that experience put her off driving for the rest of her life!

The van was an Austin Seven and it had so-called quick release wheels. These just had slotted holes that enabled wheel changes to be made without taking the nuts off of the hubs. This proved to be very unsafe, at least as far as we were concerned.

It happened like this.

One hot summer's day we set out for Joyce and Jim's wedding at Swindon. (Joyce is Olive's sister.) Olive sat in the front with Carolyn on her lap and Tony was strapped into the folding pram in the back of the van. All went well until we passed the Baths in Swindon, about to turn towards Rodbourne. Then the nearside back wheel fell off and bowled along the road beside us! As most of the weight was in the front the rear end didn't collapse suddenly but it was sharp enough to drive the tongue of a buckle on Tony's harness into his cheek, just missing his eye! Luckily the GWR Health Centre was nearby so I took Tony there to have a few stitches put in while Olive and Carolyn went on to the wedding on the bus.

The van was still operational but now only a three wheeler! We had to do something about it so Tony and I went along to a garage, or it might have been a scrap yard, and borrowed a jack and wheel brace to put the wheel back on. We arrived at the reception just a little late and more than a little dirty.

Later on, after we had saved a bit more money, I traded in the van for a steel-grey Sunbeam Talbot. Although it had a bit of body rot it was much more grand! Eventually that developed cylinder head gasket trouble and I swapped it for a huge Humber Snipe Command car. The owner of this was a recently demobbed Colonel from BAOR. He had bought the car from the unit he was serving with and had had it equipped with a hidden petrol tank which could be used by opening a changeover valve beside the driver's seat. The idea of this was (illegally) to use 'red' petrol from the hidden tank instead of the ordinary petrol in the regular tank! So-called 'white' petrol had a much higher rate of tax on it and 'red' petrol was supposed to be used only for off the road vehicles on farms and such like. I can't remember using the illegal system but that vehicle didn't stay with us very long because we found that it did less than ten miles to the gallon!

In the cottage next door to ours at Littlecote lived five German prisoners of war. Three worked for Tom Bucknell and two worked for Mr James in Froxfield. (The James' were the corn merchants in Hungerford and their farm at Froxfield bordered on Tom Bucknell's.)

Chief cook and bottle washer for the rest was Edgar Kohler who was also second cowman. Edgar was quite a mild mannered, courteous man, but he had a face like a prize fighter and he told me that he was a long time Nazi having been in the Hitler Youth! Alois Hotz was pigman and general farm worker and often had the job of driving the spade-lugged Fordson tractor which did a lot of the harrowing. The third of Tom Bucknell's men was Bernard Dobrowski, a 'colonial' German from the German minority in Transylvania. He too was a general farm worker and tractor driver.

The two who worked at Manor Farm in Froxfield were Emil Zimmerman and a tall ginger-haired chap whose name I can't remember. The last one married a Froxfield girl and when the others went back to Germany only he and Bernard stayed in England. The prisoners lived rough with only bare essentials.

Just up the road from the cottages was a wooden bungalow where two more farm workers lived. Freddie and Charlie lived with two sisters and nobody was sure whether any of them were married. The eldest woman had a daughter who was a little older than Carolyn. They all came from Romsey and were supposed to be diddykais, but nobody ever asked them whether they were or whether they were not! Freddie and Charlie did most of the stacking and thatching. They were able to supplement their meagre wages by snaring rabbits and game and in the autumn they took great quantities of mushrooms to the greengrocers in Hungerford. Their women, too, often earned money taking on hoeing the kale and mangolds and shocking up the sheaves of corn at harvest time. This could be a particularly uncomfortable job. Not only were the sheaves difficult to handle, but they were often thick with thistles and streaming wet. The women seemed to take little notice even though they usually only wore summer dressed with short sleeves!

The two leading farmworkers lived in Froxfield. Both cycled to work every day usually returning home at dinner time. Jack Povey was the foreman. He was a stocky, bluff man, full of anecdotes and very cynical about the farming ability of either his fellow workers or his employer! Jack drove the Caterpillar tractor which was used for most of the ploughing and corn drilling as well as pulling the Oliver Combine. Jack was a good craftsman. If a road or a path ran alongside a field waiting to be drilled, Jack would deliberately set out the drills at right angles to the road, simply to demonstrate to the world that at least Jack Povey could drill straight without overlapping the seams! Not only could he drill straight but he could shoot straight too. He sometimes carried a gun on his tractor and wouldn't hesitate to use it if saw a rabbit. In the absence of a gun he would stand up on the tractor and throw the short-handled paddle, which he used to clean the mouldboards of the plough! He didn't often miss! Jack's accent was broad and I had great difficulty, when I first went to the farm, in understanding what he was saying, especially when the tractor engine was running!

The other worker who lived in Froxfield was Fred Schofield. He was tall and lean and imported into the area from Berkshire with the Bucknells when they took over Littlecote Park Farm. Fred drove the long-legged Fordson Major. He did not do much ploughing and that little which he did undertake was always severely criticised by Jack Povey. His tractor work was mostly the harrowing, fertilizer spreading and general hauling. He seemed simple but he had a fair share of the countryman's natural cunning.

Quite a normal happening will demonstrate the point.

The road from the village was all uphill, and Fred often arrived late, pushing his bike up the rough farm drive. He usually claimed to have had a puncture. Come dinner time he always said that he would pump up the punctured tyre to see if it would 'hold up' until he got home! The tyre usually 'held up' and after dinner the unpunctured bike would reappear!

Tom Bucknell was a tall, lean, moustached man in his fifties. He had a slight stoop and almost always wore a sandy tweed jacket and a battered grey trilby hat with a greasy black ribbon. Apart from tending 'his wife's' chickens which were 'folded' in arks in the front field, he did no other manual work. Tom's landlord was Sir Ernest Wills, one of the 'tobacco' Wills who then lived at Littlecote House. The farm was clay on chalk with a great many large rough flints which made growing and hoeing root crops very difficult. The Bucknells were a well-known Berkshire family and Tom farmed on 'traditional' lines. The arable was mainly wheat such as Squareheads Master and the barley Sprat Archer. There was not much room for variation. Some oats were grown and the corn was followed by a grass break which was mostly ryegrass for the hay crop, which also contained a considerable amount of red clover which meant that the field could be cut again in the autumn for a clover seed crop. A further break was provided by a small acreage of potatoes and mangolds and marrow stem kale for the dairy herd.

The herd of pedigree Dairy Shorthorns were some of the best in the country and had sometimes been included in the winning teams at the Olympia Dairy Show. These were run on very commercial lines by Tom's eldest son Jim (or, as Edgar Kohler used to call him 'Yimmy'). There was another son, Michael, who was away studying geology, and a daughter, the elusive 'Gina', who was away at school and disappeared completely, as far as the farm workers were concerned, when she married Berkshire farmer Sam Pepper.

That was the farm set-up. But for Olive, virtually confined to the isolation of the farm cottage, life was a step backwards. When we moved, Carolyn was three and Tony just one year old. Olive's time was completely filled by our small family and the loneliness and low income were of minor importance. As an ex-Service Trainee my allowance was about three pounds ten shillings a week, but the Agricultural Minimum wages were not much more. We had a large garden which was much too big and too rough for our use although I was able to use the new David Brown tractor with its hydraulically mounted two-furrow plough to knock it into shape. As you can imagine, such a new-fangled bit of machinery being used by a trainee did not meet with Jack Povey's approval! We also kept a few chicken for eggs and ran some geese for Christmas. Meat was still rationed but it was permissible to keep a pig and retain half of the carcass on slaughter provided the other half was sold to the bacon factory. That half usually paid for the weaner, the food that the pig ate and was quite a satisfactory venture. The pig had to be delivered to Harris' at Calne for slaughter. This was about twenty miles away and was quite an adventure in itself. With the half of a pig for home consumption came the offal and the intestines and half the head. So it can be imagined how the house reeked of pig products of all sorts for days after! The side of bacon we hung in the empty wardrobe in Tony's bedroom.

During the fattening period the pig was kept in a sty at the back of the wash house. Feed was mainly blue dyed stock feed potatoes which were delivered in bulk in an open waggon to Hungerford Station. I can't remember exactly how we transported them back to the farm but I vaguely remember endless days bagging them up and loading them into the little Austin Seven van. These potatoes had to be boiled up and the only method of heating I had was an old primus stove. I used to boil about a half hundred weight at a time and this took a long while. One day we went to Hungerford and left the potatoes simmering on the primus. When we came back the primus had disintegrated by some sort of an explosion! Such a catastrophe was not beyond the capabilities of the ironmonger's man in Hungerford. Although everything was in pieces, including the primus tank, all was soldered together again!

One year Alois fed a pig in the farm piggery for just such a scheme. He and his fellow prisoners planned a feast! When it came to the time for slaughter the pig was brought down from the main piggery and shut in their wash house. In those days the authorities had to be notified of impending slaughter as now and a licensed slaughterman had to be employed. Being foreigners the chaps next door failed to realise this and did the job themselves! The pig was held down on the ground while one stunned it with a blow to the head with the back of a felling axe! They then cut its throat and caught the spurting blood in a chipped enamel washing-up bowl! This was too much for Alois who had fed the pig every day and had become its friend. He was so overcome with what was happening that he ran up the garden in tears!

The slaughtered pig was soon singed, scalded, cut up and turned into an endless supply of German sausages. It may have taken months to fatten but it only too a week or two to eat!

Life at Littlecote Park Farm Cottages was primitive. Bath night was quite a performance. As I said, we had no bathroom but we did have a galvanised bungalow bath which usually hung on a nail in the communal wash house. On a Saturday night it would be brought into the kitchen and all the saucepans and kettles would be ready with hot water. The children were bathed first and then Olive and I had our turn. Drainage was no problem. There wasn't any! To empty the bath the water either had to be bailed out into buckets and taken up the garden or sometimes, if it was raining, we'd drag the bath outside, taking care not to let the water slop about too much, and tip it over so that the sudsy water flooded down the back entry. God took care to wash away the suds with the rain and there were never any complaints about pollution!

At first, when we moved into the cottage, all of the cooking had to be done on the coal-fired range and Olive had all of my mother's cast iron saucepans, her flat irons and a big black kettle. When we got an oil stove we boarded up the iron utensils with the kitchen range. When we finally left the cottage they were still there. With the price such things fetch nowadays somebody must have had a windfall!

For lighting we had oil lamps. Not the old wick sort but a Bi-Aladdin pressure lamp and another table lamp with a mantle and a glass chimney. We also had an ex-RAF Aladdin heater which had been designed to de-humidify electronic equipment in aircraft. This was most successful in drying out the air in the damp cottage but the water collecting tray had to be emptied endlessly. I suppose it cost about five pounds. Quite cheap really, especially when you consider that the modern fashionable electric dehumidifiers cost in the hundreds. There was also an Aladdin Blue-flame heater on which we used to boil the water. It was this practice that nearly cost Tony his life. Tony was about two years old and this is what happened.

In the winter, after tea and before the lamps were lit, we would put a saucepan of water onto the heater ready for filling the hot water bottles. For safety, the heater was always stood in the corner of the room and the saucepan always had its handle turned into the corner as well. The children were never left alone and we thought that everything was safe. But I hadn't reckoned with Tony's playful habit of standing with his back to the wall slipping down on to his bottom and flinging out his arms at the same time. That's all he did! Alongside the heater! His arm caught the handle of the saucepan and the boiling water was tipped down his left side.

Hearing me shout out, Olive, who was upstairs came running down and, without thinking we stripped his scalding hot woollen pullover.

The skin on his arm and chest fell off in a sheet!

We were horrified!

In those days not too many people had private phones and we were certainly not on the phone. The nearest phone was over a mile away. The nearest hospital was perhaps ten miles and our doctor was at Ramsbury nearly seven miles away.

However, by this time we had our own car. Olive wrapped Tony in a blanket and all of us, Carolyn as well, piled into the car and set out for Ramsbury. I don't think we stopped to lock the back door! We were not in a state of panic but we were pretty desperate!

The passenger door could not have been fastened in our haste and slewing round the sharp corner above Littlecote, the door flew open and Olive with Tony on her lap nearly fell out! What state of mind we were in when we reached Dr. Mills' house can only be imagined. Olive took Tony straight into the surgery while I stopped outside with Carolyn. We knew that Tony's condition was serious but I don't think we realised then just how serious.

Dr. Mills immediately rang for an ambulance, and Olive told me later that he ordered hot, sweet tea for Tony to combat the shock, but I don't think that Tony had started drinking tea then and so Olive drank it! And she loathes tea with sugar in it!

When the ambulance came, Olive travelled in it with Tony and Carolyn while I followed on behind in the car, and we set off for Savernake Hospital at Marlborough, another seven or eight miles away. It was a nightmare journey for us all. The desperate urgency of the situation was magnified by the seemingly slow journey along the winding roads in the dark. Alone in the car, unable to comfort or communicate with either Olive or the children was bad enough for me, but for them, the immediate experience was not to be the end. Perhaps Tony was too young to remember very much, but he was to face months in hospital and many skin-graft operations. And the effects of the accident and particularly the journey, remained with Carolyn for years.

Tony's condition was such that we had to leave him at the hospital. We were very upset but thankful that he was being expertly cared for and we set off back to our isolated phoneless cottage. The doctors at the hospital said very little about Tony's chances and we were allowed to see him only on the one occasion. He had been all bandaged up and he was very, very unhappy. He badly wanted to go home with us. He particularly wanted to go with me to the dairy where he used to watch me milking the cows, from the safety of the cattle cake bin in the corner of the milking parlour. It seemed that the loss of this privilege most concentrated his mind in his present painful state. Nearly the whole time we were with him he sat up in bed cradling his bandaged arm, crying and rocking himself to and fro while he kept saying, over and over again, 'I want to go with daddy, I want to go with daddy'.

When visiting time was over we looked back at his ward as we walked back to the car and we could still see him rocking back and forth and crying.

The doctors at Savernake decided that a skin-grafting operation was necessary and that Tony would have to be sent to Stoke Mandeville hospital in Buckinghamshire. As they were short of staff at Savernake, Olive was asked to travel with Tony in the ambulance. She was shocked to hear from the new hospital that they had a policy of 'no visits' for children in their care. The thinking then was that the upsets caused by parents' visits were not justified. The only way they would communicate was by telephone. This meant that I had to go down to the public call box at Chilton Foliat whenever we wanted to find out what was happening to Tony. The information we were given never seemed adequate. There was delay after delay. The problem seemed to be mainly that no grafts could be carried out unless the patient was free from rashes and skin disorders of any sort. Tony kept coming out in rashes. The problem was also complicated by the fact that at that time only skin from other parts of the patient's body was used for grafts. We felt miserable. Nothing seemed to go right and the weeks rolled on.

Eventually, after three months, the grafts were complete and we were allowed to bring Tony home. We went to Stoke Mandeville and we were dismayed to find that Tony wasn't too sure of who we were! It was some miles along the road home that Tony became relaxed enough to realise that he was with his own family!

That night, when we put him to bed, I had my first sight of his injuries since the night he got scalded. The 'new' skin was far from perfect and the areas on his thighs from where the grafts had been taken were very red. But the grafts under his left arm and in his left elbow were very tight and restricted his movements. We were instructed to massage his arm with lanolin cream and strap his arm into a right-angled splint every night. All in an effort to 'stretch' out the restricting skin. There is no doubt that this treatment was most uncomfortable for him and might probably have been painful. Tony strenuously objected to the process and every night I had a distressing struggle with him.

Unfortunately all the effort proved useless, and several years later, when we were living in Devon, Tony had to go to Frenchay Hospital in Bristol to have some grafts done again. These adjustments helped a little but Tony was scarred for life. He seems to accept the position, but I'd give anything to put the clock back.

While we were at Littlecote Park Farm, Carolyn started school at Froxfield. This was about a mile away down a very narrow country road. On the first day she was there the class were given some sums to do and Carolyn, being rather bright, finished them before the other children. So, to avoid a disruptive effect on the slower pupils, the teacher thought it wise to send her out into the playground where the older children from the other class were already at play. To Carolyn, just five years old, the bigger children were boisterous strangers. So she took fright and made off home! How she managed to find her way up that lonely road with the high grassy banks and the deep, dark woods I shall never know. I suppose that these days with the increases in crimes against children such an event would be considered very risky indeed, but then, thirty or forty years ago, such events were either rare or perhaps just not reported by the media.

Carolyn normally walked to school with Sheila Black, a girl of about ten who lived in the farm bungalow. There was another child who lived nearby who also went to the village school, but he had some sort of a health problem and a taxi was provided, I think by the education authorities, to ferry him to school. The taxi could easily have taken all three but such is red tape it wasn't allowed to! How daft can you get! So Carolyn and Sheila had to trudge down the road whatever the weather. They never complained though, after all it was quite normal for country kids to walk such long distances to school.

Apart from farm staff, we didn't see many people at Littlecote Park Farm Cottages. As I said, we did get the mail delivered, and this was mostly by a man who had once worked in the Falklands and Patagonia as a shepherd. His descriptions of the cold, windy climate in that part of the world and the monotonous diet of mutton were enough to deter any would-be emigrant. It was about that time that we seriously considered emigrating for the chance of a better life for us, but both Olive and I found family ties too strong. So we didn't, in the end, attempt to go anywhere.

Our best neighbours were the Angoods at Wills' Four Winds Poultry Farm. Their house was about a quarter of a mile away across the fields and was itself a similar distance from Gamekeeper Copp's lodge at the edge of Littlecote Park itself. Their house, Four Winds, was not on a road but on a wide grassy bridle track often used, on horseback, by Mr Spreadbury, the Littlecote Estate, clerk Mr Spreadbury was one of the country eccentrics. They said that he gathered enough wool from barbed wire and brambles around the fields to spin, weave, dye and have made up into a suit! I never was able to check that out since his conversations seemed limited to the weather!

Ralph Angood at Four Winds had been in the R.A.F. during the war and had, like me, opted for the country life. Ralph kept breeds of poultry at Four Winds which have now long since disappeared. After he left, the poultry farm ceased and eventually the house itself was demolished. Both Ralph and Maude Angood came from the London area and they had one son, Malcolm, who was about the same age as Carolyn. In spite of the fact that they were near neighbours, because of the isolation, it took some time to get to know them. But when Olive had to go to hospital for operations they had no hesitation in looking after Carolyn and Tony. Without their help I would not have been able to stay at work and that would have raised some problems all round!

When we first went to Wiltshire I only got a few pounds a week, but although we didn't want for essentials, we did live pretty frugally. Days out were rare and we didn't go on holiday at all! When we got a vehicle we sometimes went out for the day.

My grant as an ex-serviceman lasted only a year and with it my job with Tom Bucknell, but this period happened to coincide with the planned repatriation of the German POWs next door. What's more, Jim Bucknell, who one would have thought would be taking over the running of the farm from his father, decided to see the world and go to Canada. These two events were about to leave old Tom in a bit of a spot! Freddie, who had been doing the relief milking, seemed to be the most likely person to take over the herd of Shorthorns from Jimmy but, for some reason or the other, Tom Bucknell asked me if I would care for the job. Well, my experience with cows was very limited indeed but at that time the idea of contract milking was being pioneered by the Hosiers and it seemed to me that if I could persuade Tom Bucknell to accept such an arrangement, for me, then that would be a chance to become self-employed.

Tom Bucknell agreed with the idea and we negotiated a rate of five pence a gallon and commission of ten percent on stock sales of heifers, cull cows and calves. In return, I was to provide all the labour necessary to look after the milking herd and the followers. Of course the other farm staff would grow the crops necessary for feeding the stock, but any time I had left after looking after my main job could be spent doing any other farm work at the agricultural rate. Of course it was more than a one man job so I had to find and pay for at least one other man.

At about that time there was a flood of refugees coming into the country from Eastern Europe and quite a number of Hungarians had been housed in the old POW Camp above Ramsbury. One of them had been told by Bernard Dobrowski that a second cowman's job might be going and so he came to see me. So I took on Alex Toth who was a man about my age and he also found a job at James' for another Hungarian, Nicholas, and so they moved in with Bernard next door.

Up till now my only bank account had been with the Post Office, but this move into the business world meant that I had to open an account with a High Street Bank. I don't remember why we chose Lloyds at Hungerford, but perhaps it was because my father had once worked at Lloyds of London!

The new arrangement caused considerable comment among the other farm workers. Freddie didn't like being passed over but nothing was ever said directly. Of course it would not have suited Tom Bucknell to offer my job to Freddie because that would have broken up the team that had been established with Charlie. Those two always worked together and they took on most of the hand hoeing and singling of the root crops on a piece work rate. This job was then used by them to provide work for their women-folk. In addition, Freddie and Charlie were the stackers and thatchers. I don't think that they were very experienced and while they thatched all of the hay stacks, it was Oliver Alexander, the professional thatcher from Froxfield, who thatched most of the more valuable corn stacks.

The system of thatching that was used in those days was this. From a load of loose threshed straw dumped by the side of the stack to be thatched, a long 'carpet' of straight straws would be drawn out. This could only be done if the heap was liberally doused with water, so a water cart had to be drawn alongside as well. When the 'carpet' had been drawn out from the base of the heap, the thatcher's mate would gather 'yealms', like straw tiles, about fifteen inches across, and place them, criss-cross, in a forked stick about four feet long, called a 'dog'.

Meanwhile, the thatcher would have prepared a supply of thatching pegs made of hazel about eighteen inches long, and spaced them in bundles, or just stuck into the roof of the stack alongside the thatching ladder. The thatching ladder was a very long ladder with the 'poles' round-side-in. This 'round-side-in' enabled the thatching straw to be lined square up against the square side, thereby making sure of a more water-tight fit between the yealms.

Lengths of binder twine, sufficient to span across the length of the stack would be wound on to a rick peg, and the ends tied to pegs inserted at intervals up the eaves of the stack. The first dog with its twelve yealms would then be placed on the roof alongside the ladder and the thatcher would commence laying the yealms, just like tiles, alongside the ladder, starting at the eaves and continuing on, up to the ridge. Each line of yealms would be secured by the runs of binder twine, in turn secured again to staggered lines of rick pegs. There would always be more pegs in the top and bottom lines than those in between because it is at those places that the winds would strike most. Working from a ladder on straw is very hard on the knees so thatchers often wore knee-pads or pieces of sacking bound round their legs instead. Each yealm had to be combed straight when it had been put in place and this was done with a 'comb' made of 6 inch nails stuck into a short piece of wood. To make the job look professional the eaves and the ridge would be secured with a straw rope made on the spot and the uneven edges trimmed with hand shears.

During my time at Littlecote Park Farm Tom Bucknell was struggling to get into modern farming gear. Although now it seems so old fashioned, I do think that Tom was, for his day, a progressive farmer. Indeed it was because of the contract milking experiment that he was asked to speak at a Dairy Conference at the Corn Exchange at Newbury. Now Tom wasn't ever such a good public speaker so, in the afternoon session, they asked me to get up on the platform with the agriculturists! It was then that my experience as an instructor in the army stood me in good stead, otherwise I would have taken fright!

But Tom Bucknell's farm was quite modern. There was a Massey Harris combine drill with a running board on the back on which the driver's mate used to ride to make sure that none of the corn spouts got blocked up with soil or lumps of wet fertilizer, and to help handle the heavy corn and fertilizer sacks from the trailer parked on the headland. Although most of the corn was cut by a tractor drawn binder, stooked, carried, stacked and threshed, we did have a combine harvester. This was a trailed Oliver with a tank. It was drawn by a tractor, usually Jack Povey on his Caterpillar. The combine man had to stand on the combine like a man at the helm of a ship with a wheel, not unlike a ship's wheel, raising and lowering the 'bed' of the combine by hand. Although the corn was held on the combine in bulk in a tank, all of it was bagged-off at intervals into four bushel West of England sacks. This meant that the combine had to pull in to a field dump whenever the tank was full. The heaps of corn often stayed in the field for some days covered with a tarpaulin, until perhaps wet weather prevented further combining. Then everyone set to loading sacks on to trailers and stacking them in the barns. There was no drier, no moisture meters and no corn sold from the field so it was necessary to be able to judge the moisture content of the grain.

We didn't have a pick-up baler although I can remember Boy Chamberlain coming up to give a demonstration with his new-fangled Ann Arbor wire tying pick-up baler. I don't think that it met with Jack Povey's approval and it required two men riding on the baler, sitting at either side of the bale chamber, whose job it was to pass the wires through to each other! This was really no different to the huge stationery baler that we used behind the thresher and for bailing the hay in winter.

All the hay that we made then was swept to a stack using a wooden sweep on the front of a tractor or an old car. Usually it was then forked by one or two men on to an elevator which took it up on to the stack to the rick-builder and his helpmates. If the hay was pitched too fast or in too big forkfulls the chaps on the stack couldn't handle it and would tend to swear a lot. Then sometimes it would stall the Lister Engine that drove the elevator or throw its belt off. Of course the engine was supposed to be an improvement on the horse gear!

If the elevator failed to go and the roof of the stack became too high the swept hay would be pitched first on to a trailer parked beside the stack, and from there to a man in a 'pitch-hole' higher up the stack. This was often done with sheaves at corn harvest, which were mostly easier to pitch, provided that the binder man had done a good job with the cutting and tying. But if the straw was short, as it often was with oats on poor land, then too often the slippery straw would slide out of the band and cascade down over the pitcher!

All this stacking of loose hay and sheaves meant that there would be long days during the winter spent in threshing corn and baling both hay and straw. The red clover seed crop, which was taken as a 'second-cut' after the hay crop in September or October, would also be swept to the stack, and threshed with a clover huller later in the year. All the baling was done with a stationery baler on iron wheels. This was pulley driven by one of the tractors, usually the Caterpillar, and required a team of four or five men to operate the system. The baler would be backed into the stack, or at the end of the thresher. Two men on the hay stack would feed the hay into a hopper which was nearly six feet from the ground. This height meant that it was easy to feed while the stack was no lower, but the last few feet of the stump was real hard work, especially when the layers of hay on the stack clung together like a heavy carpet. Not that you could feed the baler with 'carpet-like' material, indeed if you did, it was a sure way of throwing the belt off. Like the Ann Arbor mobile baler this machine required two men to tie the bales with malleable wire. It was this wire that bred a whole generation of farmers with a reputation for tying everything up with wire! Machinery and gates were often tied with wire, and there were always great heaps of tangled, rusty baler wire wherever hay or straw was fed to the stock.

Potatoes were planted, first by hand, and then with a modern 'Robot' planter, drawn by the Caterpillar, on flat land. Mangolds were planted on the flat with the corn drill, with some of the spouts blocked up. It was more usual however, to plant roots on the ridge with an old-fashioned purpose-made root drill. Grass seed was either sown by a seed-barrow pushed by hand (which was quite difficult on steepish land) or, more often, by a strange combination of a seed box mounted on an expanding hay rake. The seed box shaft was turned by a chain driven in turn by the land wheels of the hay rake, and the tines of the hay rake not only harrowed the seed in but also made a mark for each succeeding bout. I think that the patent hay rake was made by Huxtables of Barnstaple.

The system of farming at Littlecote Park Farm was pretty tight. There was always something going on. Milking all the year round, the cows being out at grass during the summer, followed by kale in the autumn and early winter and mangolds after Christmas. Hay was also fed outside in the field because there was no cow sheds and the cows had to lie out the whole time. The field work, the baling and the threshing were interspersed with mucking out the yards by hand. There were no loaders and no tipping trailers, let alone muck spreaders. All the corn was bagged and loaded by hand. Everything was done by hand!

The slackest time of the year was between hay making and harvest. But even then there was dock lifting and ragwort pulling in the pastures and quite a long of hand weeding of the bigger weeds in the corn. And, as I said, the hoeing of root crops with their masses of fat hen, red shank and mayweed was a job designed to daunt all but the stout hearted!

With hindsight there is little doubt that things were pretty uncomfortable, both physically and mentally. But I suppose that most of those who worked on farms regarded such problems as normal. Perhaps the most uncomfortable time of the year was in the autumn when the kale had to be cut with a hook and loaded onto trailers for the cows. It was normal then to get soaking wet from the dew and rain that clung to the plants, and in frosty weather we would all get chaps on our hands which would last for weeks and be most painful. Of course washing cows' udders three times a day didn't help the chaps much either!

There were perks with the job, of course. Firewood, (but no tractor drive saw-bench) two pints of milk, (probably infected with brucellosis since it was before the days when such things could be easily detected) and potatoes ... sometimes! There was Mrs Bucknell's flock of laying hens (which she kept for pocket money!) but there no 'free' eggs. Even when a nest of fifteen or twenty 'new-laid' eggs was found in a hay barn there was no reward! And the rabbits, pheasants, and hares which were taken with a mixture of stealth and skill, were, of course, just not spoken about at all! After all, Tom Bucknell was a tenant and the Wills' gamekeepers patrolled their beats with considerable regularity! Perhaps it was just that regularity which enabled those with surplus 'stock' to unload it at the back door of the 'game-dealer-cum-thatcher' down the village.

Life at Littlecote was primitive but a good introduction to agriculture for an old soldier! But it became obvious to me that if I was to compete then I would have to get some sort of intensive instruction at an Agricultural College.

At about this time Leonora's health was giving cause for concern and Gladys decided that it would be necessary to move her to her own house at Newbury. For Leonora, time was short. It had been a long, long time since she had set out with Henry on their family journey through life, and this move was to be her last. In a short while, Leonora was dead and buried with Henry at Ramsbury.

With such a strong tie to Ramsbury broken we decided that it was time to move on. I applied for a place at the Berkshire Institute of Agriculture (as the present 'College' was then called), and we left Wiltshire.

Since then the sensation of bonding with Wiltshire and Ramsbury has grown stronger. It is easy to shake off the past, if you want to, but what's the point? The families that Henry and Leonora sprang from and the many families that they have started on their own journeys have their own stories to tell and perhaps this will give them some encouragement to write it all down.

WHO LIVED WHERE

Note: The precise occupation of houses shifts over time but this list is Sid Hiscock's recollection of those families who may have lived there sometime during the period covered by "VILLAGE FOLK". Readers might care to add to this list. With dates!

1. Crown Hotel and outbuildings.
2. Cottages (Westall's - Mudge's).
3. Pear Tree Cottage (Westall's & Wootton's).
4. House (Rosier's).
5. Cottages (Duck's, Nightingale's & Chapman's).
6 & 7. House, Grocer's Shop.
8. Cottages (Withers' & Wild's).
9 & 10. Carpenter's Shop (Lawrence's).
11.
12. Hunters' Boot Repairs.
13. Hedges' (Roadman).
14. E. Hobbs' (owner of Mount Pleasant).
15. Rushen's (Woodman).
16. Westall's (Labourer) & Chamberlain's.
17. Giddings', Hiscock's, Hall's, Brown's, Vokins' & Rose's.
18. Whiting Bros.
19. Mabel Westall (Carriers).
20. Cowshed.
21 & 22. Stables.
23. Bill Watts' Blacksmith's shop.
24. Mill Cottage.
25. Miss White's.
26. Bill Watts' House.
27. Miss Waylen's.
28. a, Miss Aldridge's. b, Misses Orchard's. c, Chamberlain's.
29. Joe Alexander's (Woodman), Mrs Westall's (Widow), 'Punch' Giddings'.
30. Talmadge's.
31. Remains of a building.
32.
33.
34. Albert Angel's (Rag and Bone man).
35.
36. Watts' (Postman), Mrs Skerry's, Mr Dance's.
37. Mr & Mrs Page's.

Sid adds further notes. In 15, before Rushen's were the Pain's; in 16 before the Westall's and Chamberlain's were the Hatton's and the Jennaway's; in 19, before Mabel Westall lived Sid Watts and Family. At Mount Pleasant before the Brown's lived Mr & Mrs Hobbs. Mr. Hobbs made rush baskets and was called 'Shake pipe' because of his constant 'shakey' pipe smoking. Mrs Hobbs took snuff and would sit for hours tapping the table with her fingers. Sid says that the place reeked with snuff!

Asked to locate 'Short Pieces', referred to in the book, Sid writes: "Follow the Whittonditch Road. Go past the old Halfway House and down the hill towards Whittonditch. 'Short Pieces' is a meadow on the right-hand side."

WHO LIVED WHERE

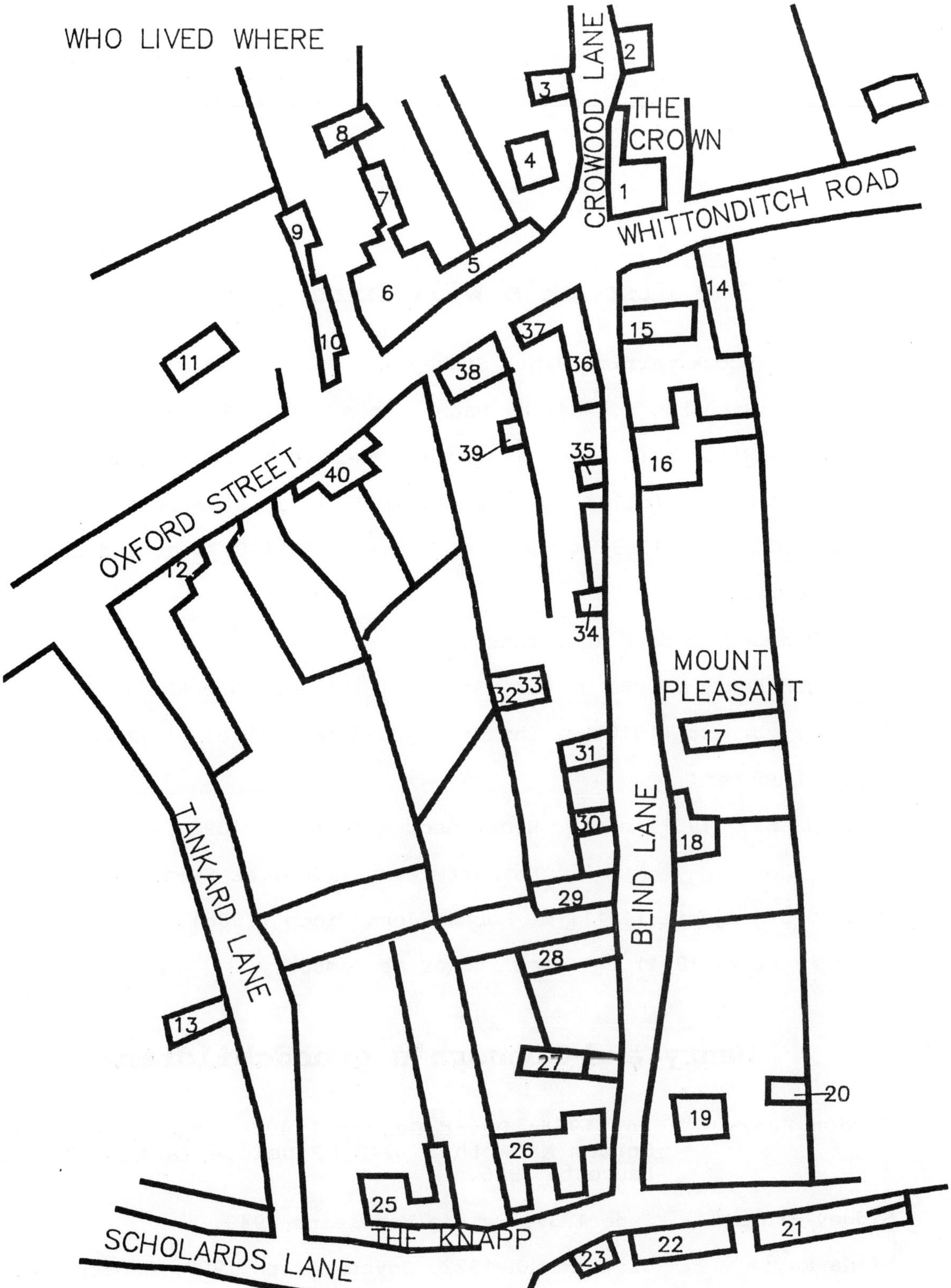

The Hiscock's Wiltshire roots.

Richard Hiscock married Sybil Stacey.

Their son Richard (c.1764) m. Hannah Powell (c.1760) at Wilsford.

Their son William (c.1804) m. Sarah Kimmer (c.1803) at Wilcot.

Their son George (c.1832) m. Eliza Smith (1838) at Wilcot.

Their son Henry (1868) m. Leonora Eliza Hobbs (1872) at Eddington.

Their sons

1. Arthur Leslie died in infancy.
2. Gordon Henry (1906) m. Mary Stanger (1913) at Knockholt.
3. Sidney Ernest (1910) m. Christine Chandler (1910) at Ramsbury.

Their daughters

1. Hilda May (1901) m. 1. Henry George Westall (1897) at Ramsbury.
   2. Herbert Perry (1901) at Swindon.
2. Gladys Marjorie (1911) m. Robert John Finch (1908).
3. Doris Esme (1914) m. James Stokes at Ramsbury.

Henry and Leonora's grandchildren.

Gordon Henry:- Ann 1935, David George 1940, Margaret Ruth 1940, Gordon MacArthur 1942, Penelope Jane 1953, Julia Laurette 1956.

Sidney Ernest:- June 1937, Sylvia Madeleine 1943.

Hilda May:- Olive Norah 1922, Joyce Eileen 1927, Geoffrey 1943.

Gladys Marjorie:- Gordon John 1935, Gerald Leslie 1936, Simon Richard 1944, Leonora Margaret 1946.

Henry and Leonora's great-grandchildren.

Gordon Henry:-	Laurence Alistair Cook, Alexandra Jane Challis (Cook), Jane Hiscock, Donna Hiscock, Sharon Elizabeth Riddle, Ashley Riddle, Stephen Gordon Hiscock, Sara Louise Hiscock.
Sidney Ernest:-	Susan Green (Greenway) Paul Greenway.
Hilda May:-	Carolyn Jane Woolley (Noble), Antony Peter Noble, Bryony Collings (Wall), Susan Buckland (Wall), Deborah Swepson (Perry), Samantha Perry.
Gladys Marjorie:-	Deborah Ann Firmager (Finch), Robert John Finch, Amanda Sue Watts (Finch), Leslie (d.) Sarah Jane Wilkins (Finch), Simon John Finch, Scott Howard Finch, Toby James Finch.

Henry and Leonora's great-great-grandchildren.

Justin Peter Haigh Noble, Zoe Louise Noble, Benjamin James Daniel Collins, Thomas Michael Stephen Collins, Sarah Jayne Buckland, Matthew James Stephen Buckland, Victoria Jayne Cook, Emma Jane Tiltman, Gary Stephen Hiscock, Matthew Paul Green, Jessica Zoe Firmager, Matthew James Firmager, Laura Jayne Watts, John Andrew Watts, Lucy Elizabeth Wilkins.

NOTE:

Through Henry Hiscock's mother, Eliza (Smith), many other family names have been traced in the Vale of Pewsey, especially in the Stanton St., Bernard and Beechingstoke area. The names so far revealed are Russ, Park, Hazel, Stevens, Dike, Neate and Tarrant. The earliest date recorded is the birth of Robert Ruddle (son of John) on 8th October 1609 at Bishops Cannings. This information was supplied by Mary Trace of Calgary, Canada, who shares a common ancestry.

WESTALLS.

John Westall married Elizabeth Levington in 1787.

Their son George (c.1806) m. Elizabeth?

Their son George (c.1824) m. Elizabeth?

Their son Thomas (1841) m. Sarah Dobson in 1857.

Their son George (?) m. Sarah Annie Wootton.

Their son Henry George (1897) m. Hilda May Hiscock.

Their daughter Olive Norah (1923) m. Leonard Noble.

Other children in each generation:

John and Elizabeth:- Richard, William, Ann, Jane, William, Thomas and Stephen.

George and Elizabeth (the second):- Charlotte, Hannah, Ann, Elizabeth.

Sarah Annie and George:- James, Edward, Lily, Louise, Elizabeth, Winifred, Emily, Edith.

Olive Norah and Leonard Noble:- Carolyn Jane, Antony Peter.

There are possible connections through the Westall line with other village names such as Appleford, Dobson, Grinnif, Harris, Messenger and Stacey.

WOOTTONS.

Henry Wootton m. Anne Garrard in 1793.

Their son William (c. 1796) m. Sarah Dobson in 1824.

Their son Henry (c. 1827) m. Betsy Marshall in 1854.

Their daughter Sarah Annie (1868) m. Henry George Westall.

Other children in each generation:-

Henry and Anne:- Charles, Edward.

William and Sarah:- John, Walter, Edward.

Henry and Betsy:- William Wallace, Fanny, Charles Edward, James, Martha, Anne.

Other village names in the Wootton family could be Axford, Berry, Dobson, Fisher, Garrard, Marshall and Woford.

FAMILY HISTORY WARNING

All links and records subject to verification!

INDEX